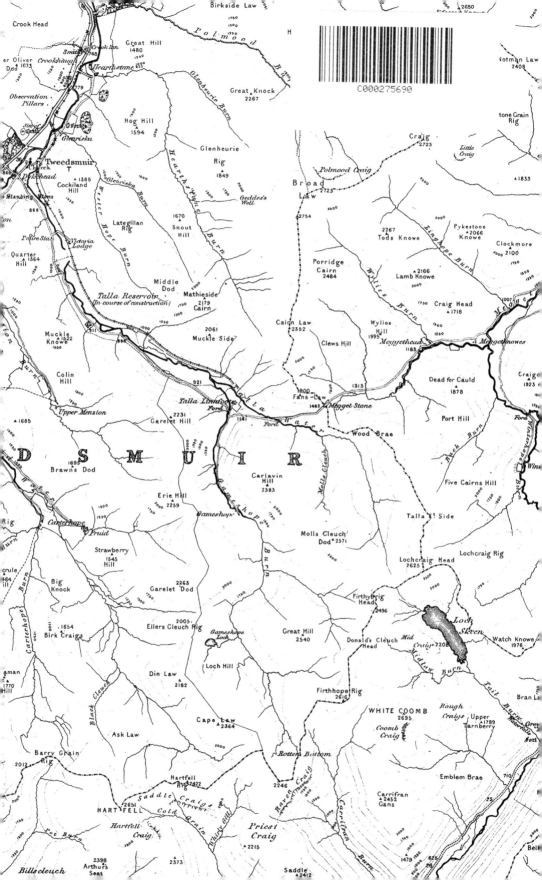

LIFE AND TIMES IN THE
UPPER TWEED VALLEY

Andrew Lorimer (1906–1996).

ANDREW LORIMER'S

Life and Times
in the
Upper Tweed Valley

Compiled by
MARGARET RAILTON

TUCKWELL PRESS

First published in Great Britain in 2001 by
Tuckwell Press
The Mill House
Phantassie
East Linton
East Lothian EH40 3DG
Scotland

Reprinted 2002

ISBN 1 86232 179 5

British Library Cataloguing-in-Publication Data
A catalogue record for this book is available
on request from the British Library

Typeset by Carnegie Publishing Ltd, Lancaster
Printed by Bookcraft Ltd, Midsomer Norton

Contents

	Colour plates	vi
	Black and white illustrations	vii
	Introduction	ix
	Acknowledgements	xi
1	My Family and Early Childhood	1
2	Tweedsmuir School	15
3	The First World War	30
4	The Upper Tweed Valley	45
5	Farming	66
6	Cottage Life	92
7	Cadgers, Moudie Men and Others	103
8	Fishing	116
9	Nature Notes	135
10	Gun Dogs	151
11	Keeping the Past Alive	160
APPENDIX 1	Poems	
	The Proposal	177
	Furnishing	179
APPENDIX 2	Miscellaneous Anecdotes	
	1 The Fiddler	181
	2 The White Cats of Over Menzion	182
	3 John French and the Partridges	183
	4 The Horned Cheviot	184
	5 Braxy Sheep	185
	6 Braid Law (Broad Law)	186
	7 Gaun Bodies or Gangrels (Tramps)	187
APPENDIX 3	A Village School in Wartime	189
APPENDIX 4	The Tweedsmuir Curling Club	195
APPENDIX 5	Register of Upper Tweed Valley Sheep Marks, 1907	200
	Index	207

Colour plates

1.1 Westwards from the Dreva Road
1.2 Ratchill Farm, Broughton
1.3 The Stobo Road
1.4 Drumelzier Mill
1.5 Looking towards Tweedsmuir and the Talla Hills
1.6 Tweedsmuir Village
1.7 Tweedsmuir Bridge
1.8 Tweedsmuir Church
2.1 Cattle at Woodend, Mossfennan
2.2 Sheep by a Woodland Burn
2.3 Herding Sheep at Stanhope
2.4 Hope Carton
2.5 Sheep Clipping at Mossfennan
2.6 Peat Cutting at Glenheurie
2.7 Watering the Team
2.8 View up Glenholm
3.1 Badlieu
3.2 Feeding the Sheep, Horseshoe Wood, Mossfennan
3.3 Shepherd's Warning
3.4 Unexpected Arrivals
3.5 The Challenge
3.6 Mother and Twins
3.7 The Tweed at Dawyck
3.8 Roe Deer in the Woods
4.1 Neidpath Castle
4.2 March Riders below Neidpath Castle
4.3 Holylee to Elibank
4.4 The Eildons
4.5 Morning View from Glentress Forest
4.6 Manor Bridge
4.7 Fruid Water before the Reservoir
4.8 The Riggs with Bell Shaw at the Burn

Black and white illustrations

Andrew Lorimer	*Frontispiece*
Hearthstane, Tweedsmuir	2
Andrew Lorimer, *c.* 1912	3
Jim Anderson with his father	5
Jumping Jack	7
Mr and Mrs Thomas Lorimer	9
Andrew Lorimer with two of his sisters, his grandmother and mother	10
Tweedsmuir School and Master's House, *c.* 1910	16
Tweedsmuir 'Side' School at Tweedhopefoot. Miss Yellowlees and pupils, *c.* 1910	17
The Martyr's Stone on John Hunter's Grave	18
Lily Bank from Tweedsmuir Bridge	21
School group, *c.* 1890, with barefoot children	22
School group, *c.* 1910. Shows 'tackity' boots	23
School group, *c.* 1918	27
Tweedsmuir Home Guard	32
Mr Yellowlees, member of the Home Guard	33
Three members of the Home Guard	36
Peat digging tools. Mr J Sharpe with his collection	37
Peat digging tools	38
Jim Lorimer, killed at the Battle of the Somme	39
The new village hall opened in 1926	41
Unveiling Day of Tweedsmuir War Memorial	42
Mossfennan House	46
Polmood, *c.* 1910	48
Kingledores	51
The Crook Inn before alterations in 1936	53
The Bield, *c.* 1910	54
Oliver	56
The road to Tweedsmuir Bridge	57
Tweedsmuir Church	58
Tweedsmuir Manse, *c.* 1910	58
The road to Glenriskie	60
Talla Water Works – opening day, 1905	61

Gameshope   62
Glenbreck   63
The Source of the Tweed   64
Drumelzier Castle   67
Clipping at Hearthstane   71
Horses and men   72
Fox shooting at Kingledores, 1917   73
Hay making. Jim Anderson and his father   81
Davie Murray with his dog and a lamb   83
John Fleming, shepherd, at the Manse Glebe   84
Thomas Lorimer and William Anderson   85
Hearthstane Cottages   96
Glenriskie   100
Geordie Bell's road-making successors in Tweedsmuir. Steam
    traction engine; roadmen   108
Waggonette at the Crook Inn, c. 1910   111
Knife-grinder   112
Stone-knapper   112
Stone dykers   113
Using the leister   117
Talla Valley before the Reservoir, looking west   118
Talla Valley before the Reservoir, looking east   119
Talla Reservoir   121
Andrew Lorimer, fisherman   123
Tweedsmuir Bridge   131
Andrew Lorimer with his pet owl   143
Andrew Lorimer with two of his spaniels   154
Curling pond, c. 1900   161
The Insh   163
Glenveg, with rowan arch at gate   167
Picnic party at Gameshope   168
Mr and Mrs Jimmy Brown   170
Mr and Mrs Millar (Mary Kerr Brown)   171
The Riggs   172
Bell Shaw at the Riggs   173
The Riggs with Bell Shaw   174
Whitekirk School, 1946. Classes 5, 6 and 7   190
Tweedsmuir Curling Club Medal, presented in 1861   196–7

Introduction

Andrew Lorimer's long life spanned almost the whole of the twentieth century. He was born in Wandel in the Clyde valley in 1906, the youngest by eight years of Thomas and Jane Lorimer's twelve children. When he was four the family moved to Tweedsmuir in the Upper Tweed Valley where Thomas Lorimer had taken the job of shepherd at Hearthstane farm. It was in this area that Andrew was to spend the greater part of his life.

Over the years he built up an encyclopaedic knowledge of the Upper Tweed Valley, its history, birds, animals and people and their way of life. Friends, anxious that this information should not be lost, implored him to 'write it down' and in his latter years, between Scottish dancing and his myriad of interests, he started to make notes, which unfortunately he never completed. When asked how he was getting on, he shyly said he was writing but was not sure how to proceed.

A few days before his death in April 1996, two weeks before his 90th birthday, Andrew arranged that all his notes should be passed on to me. I had known him for some forty years since my parents had bought a farm in Tweedsmuir. A large pile of notes, some in exercise books, others on odd bits of paper, were given to me. Andrew had written things down as they had occurred to him and often there were several versions of the same subject. These notes are fascinating and give a unique account not just of his life and times in the Upper Tweed Valley, but also of those who lived there in the latter half of the nineteenth century.

Andrew grew up in a farming community at a time when changes were already taking place in the Upper Tweed Valley. The Talla reservoir had been completed five years before and the railway track, constructed to supply the site, had only recently been removed. Many more changes were to follow over the next 86 years of his life. He had great powers of observation and an inborn ability to absorb knowledge. He knew the old herds (shepherds) who had lived in the remote glens and remembered the stories they told about the valley in earlier times. Above all he had an innate 'feel' for the countryside and the people who lived and worked there.

He attended the village school and became its first pupil to go on to Peebles High School. During this time he developed a great interest in the natural life of the valley. He explored the hills and glens and became familiar with the animals, birds and plants that were to be found there. He became, in his own words, 'addicted' to fishing and spent many hours fishing the river and burns. Old and new were blended in his life, ranging from old methods of peat digging, which were revived during the First World War, to the various methods used to catch fish from earlier times. He also became a very competent artist and his many paintings illustrate his love of the beautiful country-side around him.

When he left school he attended Moray House in Edinburgh to train as a teacher. After graduating, he taught in various schools in East Lothian until he contracted tuberculosis. He went to Soonhope in Peebles where his parents were living in their retirement and eventually was cured, but was left with scar tissue on his lungs. His first marriage in 1935 was to Barbara Cameron, a Tweedsmuir girl, and in 1938 they moved to Whitekirk in East Lothian when Andrew was appointed Headmaster of the local school. Here all his abilities were put to good use for the school and the community during the Second World War. His account of this period is given in an appendix.

In 1946 when ill-health returned and he lost his voice, Andrew retired from teaching and took over the tenancy of Mossfennan from his in-laws and where, many years before, his grandfather had been coach-man and gardener. His wife died of cancer in 1954 and two years later he married Margaret Lindsay Miller whose grandfather, James Brown, had been a herd in Tweedsmuir and whose fishing prowess Andrew greatly admired.

Andrew and his second wife remained at Mossfennan, where he ran the farm and she the guest house, until they retired in 1976 and moved to the old family home in Peebles. Here he enjoyed an active retirement growing soft fruit and combining his duties as a long-serving Elder of the Tweedsmuir Church with fishing, shooting and painting in the Upper Tweed Valley. It is not surprising that he had difficulty in finding time to write his notes.

I have compiled the following chapters from Andrew's notes, hoping they are much as he might have written them.

Margaret Railton

Acknowledgements

The following are thanked for kindly allowing reproduction of paintings, photographs and postcards in this book.

Andrew Lorimer's paintings:
Mr and Mrs J. Anderson (Broughton), Mrs G. Bateman, Mrs M. Brown, Mrs P. Fairless, Mrs D. Fortune, Mrs M. Johnston, Mrs F. Lukas, Mrs H. Maben, Mrs M. Massie, Mr D. Millar, Mrs I. Millar, Miss S. Millar, Mrs M. Milne, Miss A. Mordell, Mrs H. Nesbit, Mr P. Norris, Mrs M. Railton, Mrs M. Roper, Mrs E. Ross, Mrs M. Smart, Mr J. Smith, Mr P. Turnbull.

Photographs and postcards:
Mrs N. Anderson (Moffat), Mrs C. Chick, Dr D. Davidson, Mrs Margaret Dempster, Mr W. Guthrie, Mrs J. Johnston, Mr B. Linton, the National Museums of Scotland, Mrs M. Railton, Mrs E. Ross, Mrs M. Sharpe, the Tweedie-Stodart family.

Thanks go to Mrs M. Statham for permission to reproduce the 1907 Register of Upper Tweed Valley Sheep Marks.

The endpaper maps – OS 1″ Scotland (1904) sheets 24 (front) and 16 (back) – are reproduced by permision of the Trustees of the National Library of Scotland.

Chapter One *My Family and Early Childhood*

For understandable reasons I was never told much about my mother's near relations. My grandmother was unmarried when my mother, Jane Caldwell, was born in 1861 but married later. When she was about twelve years old my mother had to leave her home at Elsrickle in Lanarkshire and go out to work as a 'herd lassie' at Atherstane, a farm about ten miles away. By this time her mother was already widowed and greatly in need. The work at Atherstane was very hard, living conditions were primitive and food was not plentiful. She was paid twice a year at Whitsun and Martinmas when she would be allowed to go home to her mother with her £2 or £3 wages.

The 'herd lassie' had a long working day. In summer she had to have the cows in the byre ready for milking early in the morning, no matter how far away their pasture. At milking her task was to carry the full pails to the milk-house and the empties back to the milkers in the byre. After milking the cows had to be driven to their daytime field (cow-going) which was often quite a long way from the farm. At night the herd were brought in for milking again and afterwards 'caa'ed oot' to their night pasture. Atherstane had one field on the other side of the River Tweed linked by a slim footbridge suspended over the river. With great care, as it had a precarious swing, the bridge could be used when crossing to fetch the cows. When heavy rain in the headwaters brought the river down in flood, the cows had to swim across the river.

Every year a gang of potato diggers, 'tattie hawkers', came to the farm from Ireland to help with lifting the potato crop. They had to be accommodated and fed and this increased the work of the 'herd lassie' and a young boy, the 'odd laddie'. Depending on the weather, some farms employed the same Irish workers for harvesting the corn. Using sickles (heaks), one hand wielded the sickle while the other gathered the grain, dropping it when there was enough to make a sheaf. The 'bandster', usually a juvenile, made a band, laid the corn across it and tied it into a sheaf ready for stooking. Until binders came into use in the latter years of the nineteenth century, all hands were required as binders at harvest-time. Binding good sheaves took skill and experience, and this was very important to the safe storage of the

Hearthstane, Tweedsmuir.

grain. Stacking was also a highly skilled job and some stackers could 'head' their stacks so well that they needed no thatching to keep them in good condition for threshing later.

My mother used to tell of the great numbers of ants in the harvest field so that one had to watch where one sat down. When these insects became airborne they were referred to as 'fleein' emmets', and if light-coloured clothing was worn it could be black all over in a few minutes.

The social event of the year came only when the harvest had been secured and safely stacked. This was the 'kirn', a harvest home celebration with singing, dancing and recitations which continued until daybreak when the revellers made their way back to their farms in time to feed the stock and milk the cows.

In her late teens my mother went to work at Stevenston at Lyne Water and while here accepted a proposal of marriage from Jack Smith, the young blacksmith at Lyne smithy. Tragedy struck a severe blow to my mother when her intended was killed by a kick from a horse he was shoeing. His great friend, Thomas Lorimer, my future father, a young ploughman at Hamildean, was to have been best man at the wedding. He and Jack Smith had been to school together at Blyth Bridge and had remained boon companions ever since. When it was discovered that a baby was on the way, Thomas decided that it was

Andrew Lorimer, *c.* 1912.

his duty to take on his friend's responsibility, and two years later, in 1881, they were married and went to live at Dreva.

While I knew very little about my mother's relations, I was told far more about my father's side of the family. My grandfather, William Lorimer, was born in 1835 and brought up on a farm in the Sanquhar area of Dumfriesshire. He left for Peeblesshire after some family crisis and apparently had no further connection with his home county. With his wife, Mary McMorran of Wamphray, he settled at Blyth Bridge where most of the children including my father were born. Although a general farm worker, my grandfather excelled in stacking and ploughing – skills which he passed on to his five sons.

It is not known why my grandfather left Blyth Bridge to work for the Revd Dr and Mrs William Welsh at Mossfennan near Broughton. Dr Welsh was the first Minister appointed to the Free Church at Broughton and had inherited Mossfennan in 1855. Mrs Welsh was the sister of the famous Dr James Guthrie, philanthropist and founder of the Guthrie Schools in Edinburgh – the Ragged Schools. My grandfather was employed as the gardener and coachman and his family was the first to occupy the present lodge.

Mrs Welsh travelled around the countryside a great deal in her capacity as the Minister's wife and also on Free Kirk business. These journeys took her as far afield as Edinburgh, and her accurate accounts of all her main journeys show the surprising amount that had to be paid on tolls, several of which were for quite short trips. My grandfather William was therefore kept busy, and some visits necessitated long waiting periods for both horses and coachman. He described Mrs Welsh as the kindest woman you would ever meet – but not to horses.

While my grandparents were at Mossfennan their daughter, Mary, was killed in an accident on the way to school. She had been given a ride on a 'janker' (a long pole on two wheels used for carrying wood) when the accident occurred. A white stone in the roadside wall not far from the present Forest Hill marked the site.

When all his children were grown up, my grandfather moved to Wandel as grieve to Mr Black. Biggar Auction Market started while he was there and this was a project which Mr Black wished to support. My grandfather attended the first auction and was the first customer when he bought the first arrival in the ring, a young pig, for £6. Many years later, as a boy of ten, I was sent to Biggar one Saturday to buy a young pig. It also cost £6.

When he retired, my grandfather left Wandel and went to live near

Jim Anderson with his father.

Blyth Bridge. His ability to 'set' a plough was still in demand and on the nights before the ploughing matches the participants used to bring their ploughs to be prepared for the coming contest. As he had died before I was born, I knew very little about him and it was only after I started to farm at Mossfennan in 1946 that I began to hear of him from those who had known him well.

One day at the Lanark market I met two elderly farmers who, hearing the name Lorimer, discovered that I was 'auld Weelum's' grandson. They were contemporaries of my uncles and told me of their prowess at ploughing matches. They were the only competitors who could put their ploughs back on their carts single-handed.

My father was the eldest in the family and at an early age, before his parents moved to Tweedsmuir, he had started work in the smithy at Blyth Bridge. To begin with his main tasks were working the bellows and holding metal on the anvil while the smith used the big hammer. In due course he helped to fashion horseshoes and, as his first finished work, made a set of shoes for a donkey.

After a year or so he went into farm service at Cloverhill near Broughton. Here he became friendly with the three Masterton brothers whose sister married the Revd William Buchan, father of John Buchan of literary fame.

Young farm workers only stayed a year or two in any situation and kept moving to gain experience. In the late 1870s my father left Cloverhill for a new job at Hamildean at Lyne. While there he joined a group of farm lads and lassies in country dancing. Their dance floor was usually the threshing floor of the barn or, if it was not available, the wooden base of a bridge over the railway near Easter Happrew. They must have learnt a great number of dances for he later taught my sisters so well that they knew the whole range used at local dances.

Music was usually provided by a fiddler, but if one was not among the company a member played the concertina. If neither of these was available, the dancers were accompanied by the twanging of the 'Jew's Harp' or they sang the tunes or 'diddled' to them, for 'mouth music' was not, as many people believe, only used north of the highland line.

The repertoire of dances was extensive, and some with Irish names sounded as though they had been introduced by the gangs of 'tattie hawkers' and shearers who visited the farms each year. Ballroom-style dances included the waltz, polka and Schottische. Set dances like the Quadrille, Lancers, Eightsome Reels and Scotch Reels and a medley, 'Strathspey reel and Hoolichan', were all known. It was at this time

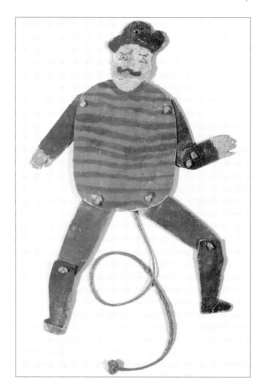

Jumping Jack.

that my father met my mother and, following the tragic death of Jack Smith, they eventually married and set up home at Dreva.

The Dreva house was the end cottage looking out over Tweed to the Dawyck woods, Atherstane and Drumelzier haugh. When my parents went to live there, certain articles of furniture were specially made for them by the local joiner. These included a baking board, a milking stool, a girnell and a dresser. Of these the dresser was the most important and could be made to specification, though most were made to a pattern favoured by the craftsman and usually reflected his own taste and skill.

James Vietch of Drumelzier had been apprenticed to a cabinet maker in Carluke and had newly returned to work in his father's joiner's shop. His first two orders for dressers were for my father and James Turnbull of Quilt Burn, a cottage at Kingledores, Tweedsmuir. They were both made to the same pattern, in two sections. The lower consisted of a two-door shelved cupboard with a set of three large drawers on top. It was about six feet wide and two feet deep, capable of holding all necessary kitchen ware. The top was not so deep and had a line of smaller drawers with shelving above with pillars ending in turned finials. The fronts of the drawers etc. were made of mahogany, and also the round, handmade handles on the doors and drawers. All the joints were perfectly dovetailed and the drawers moved and fitted with an excellence born from a craftsman's love of his work. After a lifetime of hard use this piece of furniture was as perfect as if newly made.

The girnell, a wooden cupboard, was made with an internal partition providing separate sections for the dry storage of flour and oatmeal. A girdle was also a much-used necessity and was often smithy-made though, like pots and pans, it was sometimes bought from a local ironmonger. These moveables ('swees') were the property of the cottagers and were taken with the rest of their furnishings when moving house. Such cherished possessions were always kept in shining condition and were a mark of a conscientious housewife.

If farmwork was well forward in late summer, my father was dispatched with a cart and a pair of horses to Megget where relations of Lindsay, the farmer at Dreva, occupied high-lying sheep farms. These farms depended entirely on hay to keep their flocks over winter and my father helped the shepherds to get in their winter fodder. He enjoyed this contact with the scattered households, many of whom were related by blood or marriage. Hoggs, Laidlaws and Shiels predominated and most had long traditional ties with the glen.

One of the incidents which happened when my parents were at Dreva was the big flood of 1884 which swept parts of the wooden bridges which crossed the Tweed further up the valley down on to the Drumelzier haughs. Another occurrence which affected life in the district about this time was the great snowstorm of 1890 which was accompanied by a period of severe frost. Megget and Yarrow sheep were fed on the thick ice on St Mary's Loch but those further up the glen were driven across the hills into the Tweed valley in reach of hay.

Lindsay of Dreva had an interest in Cramalt and Meggethead and the stock had been 'evacuated' to Tweed. My father set out with a cart loaded with hay up the Tweed road. After negotiating heavy drifts he got within sight of the Crook Inn when he was stopped by deep drifts, piled up between the walls at either side of the road. Above the road on the hillside the wind had blown most of the snow away and made it possible to continue a bit further. But no gate was available to make a way through, so the dyke had to be demolished to make a gap. He managed to get the load through the gap and had gone a short distance along the hillfoot when the sheep appeared where

Mr and Mrs Thomas Lorimer.

Andrew Lorimer with two of his sisters, his grandmother and mother.

Glenveg now stands. The animals were so exhausted and hungry they were not driven to Dreva but fed where they were until a change in the weather made it possible for them to return to their home pasture – which they did with surprising haste.

Some of my brothers and sisters were born at Dreva and when old enough went to school at Drumelzier. In term-time this entailed quite a long walk every day by Merlindale Bridge. Occasionally in summer they waded along the river in low water which almost halved their journey. This was before the reservoirs were built further up the valley and the Tweed carried some five or six times its present volume of water.

Life was always hard for my parents. Rearing a family involved both parents and my mother worked in the fields at all the busy periods of the farming year – harvest, turnip singling and shawing, and haytime. They had a cow of their own and would rear a pig for ham. My mother had tremendous stamina and could accomplish an enormous number of tasks with apparent ease. She used to tell of the worry of being in debt to a colporteur (travelling salesman) for their large family bible which was being paid for by instalments. Nevertheless these were good times as well as bad.

When my grandfather retired from his post at Wandel, my father succeeded him there and when the farmer, Mr Black, died he stayed on under Mrs Melville. When she gave up farming, my father took a house in Roberton (Kilpotlees) and started general work as a freelance. In this capacity he took a drainage contract at Hearthstane farm in Tweedsmuir where he lodged with one of the shepherds and walked back to Roberton at weekends. While there one of the herds took ill at a critical time of the year and my father took over the herding very successfully until the shepherd recovered. When a vacancy for a shepherd occurred, my father was asked to take his place.

My parents moved to Hearthstane in Upper Tweedale in 1910 where my father was one of three married shepherds. This was in the parish of Tweedsmuir which included all the headwaters of the river and was ringed by a semi-circle of the highest hills in the Southern Uplands. At the farm two of the shepherds' houses were built in one unit with both doors side by side. I was now four years old, born in 1906, the youngest of the family of 12 (6 boys and 6 girls) by 8½ years. By great good fortune our neighbours, the Andersons, had a boy of my own age. Jim and I became inseparable playmates, sharing most of our activities and even some of our interests.

My earliest memories before we came to Tweedsmuir are very faint. In Tweedsmuir, however, I have a clear picture of some of the celebrations of the coronation of King George V and Queen Mary in 1911. Games were held and even we very young children were expected to take part in races. My own understanding of the instructions must have been a bit hazy, for when I got in front I stopped to wait for the others and became all the more confused with people shouting for me to go on. I don't remember the result but I do recall the blue coronation mug and the coin, a five-shilling piece, which we each took home. My mug, with pictures of the King and Queen depicted on the side panels, was never used and was kept as a memento safely on a high shelf of the kitchen dresser. Another memory of that occasion was of seeing a young man coming in to win a race to the top of a nearby hill and back.

Christmas was not celebrated in those days nearly as much as now. It was regarded only as a children's festival with little exchange of gifts among adults. One particular Christmas was memorable to both my playmate Jim and myself. As money was always in short supply and bought toys hardly thought of, my father decided he would make us something for our stockings. Working when we boys were safely in bed, he cut out figures from strong cardboard. These he made into identical jumping jacks with jointed arms, legs and head controlled by a master string. When this was jerked sharply all the moving parts behaved in an erratic and, to us, amusing way. The brightly coloured, cheerful faces looked out from our stockings, hung near the fire for Santa's convenience, on Christmas morning, and, with perhaps an apple or a few sweets, made us quite happy. The jumping jacks were made to be hung up so that they could be seen and activated in the passing. Mine stayed with me for many years and eventually was given away. Jim's, on the other hand, was not so hard-worked and was still in almost pristine condition over 80 years later.

Our two households at Hearthstane both had a resident grandparent. Jim had his mother's father while we had my mother's mother. Jim's grandfather looked after the cattle on the farm and the garden at the big house. He was a large, strong-looking man and claimed that his good health resulted from his diet. Instead of porridge he always took 'brose'. This was made by putting oatmeal in a bowl with a lump of butter and pouring boiling water over it. A plate was then laid on top to keep the steam in, and when sufficiently cool it was eaten like porridge but often with buttermilk instead of milk. In spite of his apparent health and stamina he was one of the first victims of the famous (or infamous) 'flu epidemic of 1918.

My grandmother, who by this time was very old, also had some peculiar tastes in food. She was extremely fond of curries, and when others might use salt or pepper she used curry powder. She often helped my sister Janet with her dressmaking and needed no spectacles as her eyesight was as good as it had been in her youth. I always remember her small, upright figure with a shawl round her shoulders. Some of her old Scots words and sayings remind one of our heritage that has died from neglect.*

---

* Some of Granny's words:

'fikie' (as applied to work), something which needed too much attention to detail;

'feck', the most of a number, a majority;

'hansel', wear for the first time (for good luck a new garment had to have a coin in the pocket);

'hain', to save or not use much;

'fyle', dirty or to make dirty;

'flyte', to scold;

'taigle', go slowly or be kept from moving fast;

'taim', empty;

'hantle', a reasonable amount, a good deal;

'thole', bear, put up with;

'treffy', handful (one hand);

'gowpen', double handful.

In those times when cooking was on open fires, holders were needed when handling hot pots and pans. Granny would make what she called 'peesweeps' whenever she found odd pieces of material. These she folded and cut out into the shape of pewits, beak and all. Sewn together, with beads for eyes, these protected the hands though they often looked too nice to use.

Isolated from communal games and play, country children had to fall back on their own initiative for their amusement. Toys and other playthings were practically unknown and we didn't play ball games. The fast-running water of the nearby burn was a favourite spot, and here we had our swing suspended from a branch partly overhanging the water. We could mount onto the seat on dry land but thereafter we swung out over the fast-running stream. This added to the thrill, especially as dismounting could mean tumbling down into the burn if your timing was faulty.

Much of our play was centred on the occupations of our fathers. Both Jim's father and mine were shepherds on the same farm, and our ambition as small children was to share in their work. To this end we invented a game which was a unique form of play. On a bare but grassy knoll behind the cottages we laid out small stones of similar size in continuous lines to form a complete plan of a sheepfold. Jim was the prime mover in the project for, from his earliest days, he was intensely devoted to the black-faced sheep which his father herded and could identify certain members of the flock with complete accuracy. He was a 'guid kenner', the Lallans term for someone with this most useful gift.

Our sheepfold followed the design of that at the back of the farm steading and, with pieces of moveable wood for gates, included a dipper with drying pens, a shedder which could be used to separate sheep into different categories, and a clipping (shearing) area with the appropriate pens for each class of sheep being shorn. For sheep we had smooth regular stones from the nearby burn with white quartzes for lambs which, in our imagination, trotted behind their solicitous dams. So we simulated the main sheep handlings like shearing, dipping and speaning (weaning), each requiring different movements through the maze of buchts (pens). If, however, a wrong movement occurred, the whole set up came to a halt and meant the game had to go back to the beginning.

It was quite a difficult and instructive game in which Jim became expert, but I was apt to desert in favour of more exciting pursuits.

The fold stayed intact even after we had started school. It gave both of us a unique preparation for real herding which Jim started immediately after leaving school, finally farming his own stock of over 1,000 black-face ewes. At 88 he still looked after a flock near his home, attending them with his dog at least once every day.

It was about this time that the *Titanic* disaster occurred and the newspapers were full of details of the tragic event, including the account of the band playing and the passengers singing the hymn 'Nearer my God to Thee'. Hearing these items of news being discussed by our elders had a strong influence on our immature imaginations and Jim and I decided to re-enact the disaster.

Behind the Hearthstane cottages water used to gather in a hollow in the hay field next to the drying green. Though very young, we were allowed to play there as the water was only about 1½ to 2 feet deep. It seemed an ideal spot in which to re-enact the disaster. Our *Titanic* was made from a raft which included an old wash tub. We got into this and by pushing back on the ground with a clothes pole our ship moved a foot or two into the pool and immediately started to sink slowly to the bottom. This was the cue for us to start singing 'Nearer my God to Thee' to the best of our childish abilities. Unknown to us, the launch and the 'disaster', as well as the audible accompaniment, had been witnessed with much amusement by Mr Thorburn (the owner of Hearthstane) and his daughter Nancy, who later told our parents the reason for our wet clothes. Neither Jim nor I was allowed to forget this incident nor were we able to forget the *Titanic* disaster which prompted it.

Chapter Two   *Tweedsmuir School*

Enrolment at the Tweedsmuir school was compulsory at the age of five and was supposed to occur on two dates, April 1st or the first day after the summer holidays. My birthday came in May, but as my friend Jim had a February date of birth and joined on April 1st 1911, I went along too, though officially slightly under age.

There were about thirty pupils in the school. Jim and I had only a moderate mile and a half walk to school but most of the pupils had two or three miles, and one girl had at least five miles. The very young children were often too tired when they arrived to concentrate on their lessons.

The school buildings followed the early nineteenth-century pattern. One large room was divided by a space the width of two double desks. From the Master's knee-hole desk in the front the lines of pupils' desks rose in steps to the back wall. There was an open fireplace at each end where, in wet or snowy weather, pupils were allowed to dry their clothes.

Most of the children wore tackety boots with the tackets (nails) in lines with steel toe plates and heel plates. Some wore clogs with wooden soles shod with 'cadkels', which looked rather like horses' shoes. The summer months were barefoot time when boots and stockings were discarded. One of the benefits was that we did not have wet feet and could wade anywhere we wanted. As the stony roads made hard walking, we usually followed grassy cart roads and unused tracks where the walking was softer.

Some pupils had oilskins and sou'westers but wet footware was common as no-one had wellingtons at that time. Disasters occasionally occurred when drying in front of the school fires as over-heating or burning destroyed stockings and even boots, but anything was better than putting on soaking garments. Boots were coated with sheep fat, and 'hoggers', old stockings without feet, were put over boots and tied at the bottom to keep out the snow. After World War I puttees were sometimes used.

The rectangle in front of the school was covered with gravel with the remainder covered with fairly rough grass. There were separate girls' and boys' porches and covered sheds. The toilets were situated

some way behind the main building on either side of a wall running
to the bottom of the playground. In the playground stood a tall,
tapering flag pole. This, and another at the Manse, had been made
from tall trees from the Hearthstane woods in 1911, Coronation year.
On Victoria Day (May 23) and other royal occasions the whole school
turned out to make the appropriate patriotic demonstration.

The schoolhouse, standing between the school and the Talla road,
had recently been enlarged and a fence built and trees planted to cut
off access to the very steep and dangerous rocks of the deep and murky
Linn Pool.

Inside the school one side of the classroom was used all the time
and the other for special classes like knitting and sewing. Decoration
on the walls was entirely absent except for a small framed list of 'Dux'
pupils going back for many years. In addition to the Master's desk
and chair, and the blackboard, there was a rack of shelves full of
books with a small brass plate indicating that it had been presented
by Andrew Carnegie. Latterly a travelling library changed the books,
or at least some of them, perhaps twice a year.

Unseen in a locked drawer in the Master's desk lurked the dreaded
tawse. Misdemeanours like talking, laziness, lateness, carelessness, continuous mistakes and misbehaviour outside school could be dealt with
by application of the 'belt', as it was sometimes called. The one good
point about this was that it was quick and, if not soon forgotten, was
at least not dwelt on and carried little disgrace.

Tweedsmuir School and Master's House, c. 1910.

Tweedsmuir 'Side' School at Tweedhopefoot. Miss Yellowlees and pupils, *c.* 1910.

Some years before a 'side school' had been opened further up the valley at Tweedhopefoot to cater for children living too far away to attend the main Tweedsmuir school. The green tin hut consisted of a single room where some ten or twelve children were taught. At one time most of the pupils came from one large family living at Tweedhopefoot.

My first schoolmaster was elderly Mr John Yellowlees. His family was grown-up and, as his wife preferred to live in Peebles, his daughter Janet kept house for him, taught sewing and knitting and helped out at the Tweedhopefoot school. When Mr Yellowlees retired Mr Peter Allen was appointed and his wife took over Miss Yellowlees' work.

In addition to the schoolmaster there was another appointed official. Mr G Curry, the local tailor ('stitch') and postmaster, was also the attendance officer or 'whipper-in'. His function was to make sure that all school-age children attended regularly. I don't think he was ever really needed as truancy was unknown though, of course, irregular attendance was sometimes unavoidable.

The School Board and not the Education Department controlled school life to a great extent. Nevertheless once a year the Inspector, a fearsome figure, came and put us through our paces. Much overawed on these occasions, our oral work suffered though I remember once we got talking about hill plants and especially cloudberries and where they grew. A date was set when they would be ripe and in due course a small quantity was gathered from the Garelet and sent to H.M.I.

Early memories of school include using slates and 'skealy' (chalk) for figures and writing. Jotters and pencils came in within a couple of years, and when we could be trusted with pen and ink another book with better lined paper was provided. Our writing had to follow the fixed style of a copybook using nibbed pens and ink from an inkwell inserted in the desk top. In awkward and inexperienced fingers, ink had a habit of reaching the paper erratically, producing irregular and blotchy attempts at the art of calligraphy. One occasion remains vividly in my memory when I was severely reprimanded when spots of rain, blown through a high window, spoilt a whole page of writing.

Most young entrants arrived at school with little knowledge of vocabulary or numbers though some had already learnt the alphabet and a few numbers. One method of counting which was not on any

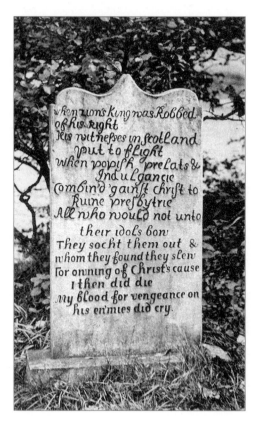

The Martyr's Stone on John Hunter's Grave.

curriculum was practised by shepherds' children when they were quite young. This counting was in fives and involved the use of fingers, with one unique advantage that you did not count above 20. This went 5, 10, 15, 20 and then the score was noted by turning down the small finger on one hand. This was repeated and the next finger was moved. When the thumb completed the full hand (5 score or 100), it was transferred to the small finger of the other hand and the count of the second and following hundreds continued with the full hand reaching 25 score or 500, which was the standard hirsel (flock) for one shepherd.

Somehow I have few memories of in-school activities but enjoyed learning a great deal of poetry, especially screeds of Scott's 'Marmion' as well as other Scott poems like 'Lochinvar' and, of course, some Burns. We learnt music by ear with songs like the 'Rowan Tree', 'Scots Wha Hae' and the 'Canadian Boat Song'. There were numerous hymns, paraphrases and psalms which were produced when the Minister, the Revd W S Crockett, came to the school. On these occasions I particularly disliked having to recite the verses on John Hunter's grave in the Tweedsmuir churchyard, known as the Martyr's Grave. I still cannot remember more than a line or two and, for some reason, I detested the rest.

I don't remember being taught to draw but I recall scratching in the red sandstone of the Crook Brae bridge a fair representation of a cuckoo which had obliged me by posing on one of the railway fence posts. I also remember one occasion when we went outside the school to draw the view looking over at the old hall. We later painted in these fair-sized drawings and two were shown to the Hall Committee who were then planning a new hall. To my chagrin my special friend's painting was chosen, framed and hung in the old hall and later transferred to the new hall.

While the girls were taught both needlework and knitting, the boys also had to learn to knit, for that skill was much practised among shepherds. One reason was that they were often partly paid in kind by having a 'pack' of their own. A pack was usually a score or half a score of ewes from which the wool as well as lambs and mutton accrued to the shepherd in lieu of cash. The wool, which provided much of a family's clothing, was processed by certain mills and could be made into knitting wool or manufactured into tweed. The tweed patterns were limited and the cloth itself was so substantial that it didn't wear out before the clothes were outgrown and so they were passed down to younger members of a family.

Once when a new keeper came to Kingledores and his two children attended the Tweedsmuir school, it was discovered that they had come from Aberdeenshire where the boys were not taught knitting. Jamie, a boy of nine, had to start from scratch and Miss Yellowlees had to give him much individual attention. After one long session one of his class mates asked him how he had got on. 'No bad if I could keep them loops frae comin' off the wyers' was the reply. From then onward he was 'Jimmy loops' to all his fellow-knitters.

One progressive dominie (master), Peter Allen, thought it would be a good thing to teach us all to swim. The Carlowes Bridge area was looked at but the rocks and deep water made it too dangerous for swimming lessons. Instead a suitable pool at Talla Burn was chosen. The method intended was to have a harness on our shoulders which was attached to a long shaft held by the schoolmaster himself. The water in Talla Burn came straight from the depths of the reservoir which in turn was fed from deep, cold underground springs. Even though the sun was shining, the water was ice-cold, the budding swimmers became shivering wrecks and the project had to be abandoned hurriedly. Some of us taught ourselves to swim but in my case, though quite efficient, the style was unique and ungainly.

Both girls and boys took part in games and, except in really bad weather, these were played in the fresh air. Playground games included various forms of 'tig' (touch) and were played on the gravel in front of the school building. 'Smuggle the geg' was played on the long, sloping, grassy rectangle down the side of the school. Two teams were picked to include everyone from the largest to the smallest child. One team formed a line across the narrowest part while the other remained at the top. The 'geg' was an agreed object which was small enough to be concealed by the smuggler whose identity was unknown to the opposing team. The object of the game was to smuggle the geg through the opposing line and reach the lower boundary line. Those on the defending line had to try to stop and capture the player carrying the geg. This could be quite a rough game and would have been good training for the rugby field. If the wrong player was tackled, the geg 'smuggler' could slip through to the boundary when the teams then reversed places.

Out on the hill, near the Menzion and Talla roads, a complete circular groove marked the track of the rounders game which was played by all ages. The ball was usually an old tennis ball, the bat any bit of wood wide enough to hit the ball, and the bases were marks dug into the turf. The rules were the same as for baseball though our game was far removed from its American counterpart. This summer game had but a short season for when it rained the track became too slippery.

'Kick the Can' was a hide-and-seek game with the addition of high-speed attempts to reach the can, but the kicking did not improve the ends of our boots. 'Hares and Hounds' gave us miles of hard running on cross-country courses over obstacles which we thought might daunt or delay the pursuers.

In wet, snowy weather we were more or less confined to the covered sheds which adjoined the cloakrooms. The girls could skip in their own side but the boys only joined in when skipping was outside. Games involving marbles were played by both boys and girls and also an unusual indoor game called 'Bannety'. This involved rolling a ball into bonnets (caps) arranged on the ground along the wall with the peaks turned outward. Not everyone had suitable headgear and I, like some others, had to borrow when it came to my turn.

When the curling pond froze over, as it always did at least once each winter, sliding became the popular sport. When the ice began to melt it remained solid in the middle but a strip of water appeared at the edges. To reach the solid ice we had to jump over this water barrier, which was fairly risky. When too many people had crossed, the ice began to sink, the sliding had to stop and we had to make our way to terra firma as best we could.

Lily Bank from Tweedsmuir Bridge.

As it was too far for most of the children to go home for lunch, they brought 'pieces' with them but nothing to drink. Our pieces were usually plain bread from the baker's van, the scotch variety with crust on top and bottom. The bakers also carried cookies and a few cakes which were referred to as 'small bread'. All the housewives baked scones on girdles, the rounds cut to form four triangles. Some had ovens where scones could be baked without being turned. Pancakes (dropped scones) containing egg were made on the girdle, and sometimes currants were added as a special treat.

Quite near the school there was a small shop in a long cottage-type house called Lily Bank. Here sweets and biscuits could be bought and adults could obtain cigarettes and tobacco at a tiny counter with a few shelves on the wall behind. The shop was run by a very elderly lady and on her death it was carried on by her niece who added pencils and rubbers to the stock. Money for sweets was scarce and some families never patronised the shop. The meagre stock included Archibald's Battleaxe Toffee, Rowntree's Clear Gums, Abernethy Biscuits, Striped Black Balls, and sometimes Chocolate Walnuts which, at 2d each, were too expensive for children to buy.

One of the special days at Tweedsmuir school was the day of our annual excursion to Gala Burn Wood. Every year in late spring or early summer a day was chosen to coincide with the blossoming of

School group, c. 1890, with barefoot children.

School group, *c*. 1910. Shows 'tackity' boots.

the primroses and the glen violets. It was not a highly organised outing but rather a spontaneous celebration of nature. The wood was a good mile away, sometimes the small children were left at school, and those who did go had to be fit enough to run most of the way, both there and back.

Gala Burn Wood was reached by a route that took us up the bank of the Tweed for half a mile and then up Gala Burn and over the road into the wood itself. This consisted of a mixture of mature trees, widely scattered, through which ran the tumbling waters of the burn. I particularly remember a clump of silver-leaved aspen near the gate which flickered and rustled as we passed. The trees were not too dense, and enough light got through to allow grass and flowers to grow, especially clumps of yellow primroses beside the burn. The boys climbed trees, some to reach birds' nests and some just for the sake of climbing. The girls followed the burn with its little waterfalls and gathered bunches of flowers from its banks.

It was on one of these visits when I was first allowed to join the expedition that I saw a woodcock in its nest in the nook between the roots of a spruce tree. I did not discover it myself but was shown it as a great favour by one of the older boys who was a keen naturalist. Stopping me within easy view, he told me where to look. At first I could see nothing but eventually I became aware of two dark eyes and the round top of a bird's head. The rest of the bird was undetectable as it blended so well with the surrounding brown leaves. In my excitement I pointed toward the nest and in a flash the bird took off, leaving four brown eggs hastily covered with loose leaves.

Without much in the way of formal exercise we managed to keep quite fit. The long walk to and from school was usually exercise enough, but sometimes for younger pupils it was rather too much. Fruid was five miles away, Glenbrec was three, Patervan, Kingledores and Talla Linnfoot about the same. Kingledores Hopehead was less but the route came over the hill and involved quite a climb as well. Hearthstane and Crook were a mere mile and a half from school and there was a choice of three routes which Jim and I could follow.

We could take the farm road which crossed the Tweed by the strong wooden Hearthstane bridge and follow the main Moffat road all the way to Tweedsmuir. In good summer weather when we travelled barefoot we followed a path from our homes which joined the little-used farm track to Glenriskie which continued past the Kirk and on to school. These tracks consisted of wheel ruts between which were grassy ridges which were kind to our bare feet.

The third route was the most interesting and one which we often took. This left the main road at a cutting which joined the unused Talla railway line and then crossed the aqueduct which carried water from the Talla reservoir over the Tweed to Edinburgh. Here we joined the 'barefoot' track and so on to school.

At certain times of the year, especially in winter, the early morning sun poured down from behind Broad Law through the glens and across the road in wide warming beams, while the ridges cast cold shadows. The children on their way to school found alternative stretches of sun and cold shadow. On such days the very small children were placed between two older children, hand in hand, and in the cold stretches they ran with the little children's feet hardly touching the ground. On the sunny parts they could get as much warmth as possible. There were three stretches of sun and three of shadow on the way to school, ending with the sun spreading out down the wide Talla glen.

Returning home after school was much less exciting, for by then the sun had sunk behind the continuous ridge on the west side of the valley. Although we returned in shadow, it was not usually so cold as in the frosty morning and there was always a sense of urgency to reach home with its promise of food and warmth.

An incident one morning brought us into visual contact with an otter. This was the morning of an annual event, the ice flood which carried away the accumulated ice of the winter frosts from upper Tweed and particularly from Fruid Lakes. Throughout the prolonged frosts the waters of the Lakes had become slower and eventually froze to form great sheets of thick ice which covered the whole area. When the thaw came this ice, combined with that from the frozen headwaters of the Tweed, formed a flood which could take half a day to pass. At Carlowes Bridge at Tweedsmuir this was an awesome sight accompanied by continuous crashing and grinding from the rocks below.

On the morning in question this flood was at its height with the whole river a heaving, grinding mass of pieces of ice of every shape and size. On the bank opposite to us a large and very agitated otter was travelling upstream, parallel and close to the tumbling ice but afraid to enter the water. Once or twice he tried to plunge in only to turn away, and eventually he went into an adjoining field. Spellbound, Jim and I watched him with his galloping gait and clumsy-looking rudder, which in the water was his chief asset but on land was an encumbrance swinging from side to side. At the deep drop into the nearby Bield Burn he disappeared and, as he did not reappear on the other side, I presumed he followed the bed of the Burn and would find a safe hiding place for the rest of the day. The other children had gone on ahead to school and were, by now, out of sight. I, however, had started on the trail of one of the most interesting and least understood citizens of our Tweedsmuir waters.

Sometimes we were kept off school if the snow was too bad, and once or twice we were sent home early as conditions deteriorated. Wading through snow could be most exhausting but it provided added interest to the journey to school as each day the snow recorded every track of the otherwise secret movements of the various animals: rabbits and hares to their nightly feeding grounds, stoats and weasels searching along the walls, tiny mouse tracks from one refuge to another and, looking over Carlowes Bridge, the otter trails up the rocks beside the burn. I could recognise these tracks and follow the animals to their lairs.

Among these tracks were also paw-marks. One set of these which started at the Manse showed how the Minister's tom cat, in excursions far afield, visited the scattered households of the parish much more frequently than the reverend gentleman himself. At the Sunday School party a word game called 'The Minister's Cat' was a hardy annual – he was a very popular cat.

One aspect of country life which interested most children was the calls of wild creatures, especially birds. It naturally followed that many made attempts to imitate them. Successful mimicry meant evoking responses from the birds themselves. To produce the calls of the cuckoo, owl and pigeon required the hands to be pressed together, palms inward and fingers closely intertwined, leaving only a slight space between the thumbs. By blowing into this aperture the hooting sounds could be so accurately reproduced that dialogue was frequently established at the first attempt. On one occasion a cuckoo objected so much to my mimicking an unseen rival that he flew on to the top of the flagpole in the school playground shaking his outspread wings and puffing with rage.

The various calls of the curlew, the peewit and the golden plover could all be produced by mouth like whistling, which boys practised naturally as a necessity for every budding herd. The corncrake, perhaps the most elusive and seldom seen of our migrants, invited mimicry yet, even though one could effect dialogue, there was little or no chance to see or approach the owner of the unique scratchy voice.

The crow family - rook, jackdaw, hoodie (carrion crow) and raven - had a whole language ranging from the light 'kee' of the jackie down to the deep, harsh 'krrk' of the raven. Each had numerous variants covering many different meanings. The ravens which inhabited the crags of Talla and Moffat Water usually left every morning flying northwards at a great height and returned towards nightfall. They could be seen against high white clouds but, if the clouds were low, they could only be seen crossing the openings in the sky.

Animal calls, like the squeaking of the mouse, the distress call of the rabbit when attacked by a stoat, the bleating of a lamb or a ewe, were all subjects for mimicry and also for interpretation. Although foxes have several calls, they are most easily attracted by using the noises of animals associated with their prey. I was always thrilled by the whistling of the otters but to succeed in communicating with them the pitch and modulation had to be just right and then they could be encouraged to come quite close. As an example of successful mimicry I recall one incident which occurred on Carlowes Bridge late one moonlight night. An otter whistled far down below the bridge and I started answering. It responded and came nearer and nearer until it

School group, *c.* 1918.

reached the rocks in midstream below the pool and climbed into view on a flattish rock. Sadly the spell was broken when my companion whispered 'I see it' too loudly and the otter disappeared.

In late summer and early winter there were days when some of us spent all our available time watching trout, sea trout and salmon ascending the rocks at the Tweedsmuir Bridge. Hanging uncomfortably over the stone parapet of the bridge, we watched fish leaping with varying success up the white spouting water which fell several feet into the whirling pool (lynn) below. Smallish trout were prone to accidents, sometimes killing themselves on the rocks. When the Tweed was in flood, the fish could pass up the fall without having to jump, and when the river was too low they made no attempt to travel.

In recent years the lower fall, which was then the main leap, has almost disappeared. The rock has worn away and where there was a clear drop of white falling water, a mere slide between the rock walls now allows the passage of fish without any need to leap.

In midsummer the lynn again became a place of interest. For a day or two numbers of squirming, miniature eels attempted to climb the wet rocks below the fall, using clumps of wet moss to get holds on the way. Evidently the rush of the falling water prevented them from getting up the main fall, so they climbed over the moss on the rocks to avoid this obstacle.

Grouse shooting played an important part in our lives as our services were needed as beaters. Heathery farms with good stocks of birds were looked after by full-time keepers, and grouse were driven to lines of well-built butts. Early in the season, beginning August 12th, extra beaters were needed and sometimes teams of between 12 and 20 swept round the contours of the hills in evenly spread lines with flags waving.

August became a busy time when, like all the other local children (girls often as well as boys), Jim and I were employed as beaters. When I first started in 1913 the pay was 3/6d per day but by the end of the 1914–18 war this had increased to 5/– per day. Jim and I would act as beaters nearly every day of the summer holidays and, like the other children, earned enough money to buy boots and winter clothes. Families came to depend on the shooting season for considerable help with their household budgets. The Tweedsmuir school holidays were delayed so we could have a longer beating season, which was sometimes useful if the game were late in maturing because of the weather. The children benefited in health and fitness and, in my case, I gained a detailed knowledge of all the hills, glens and burns as well as the birds, insects and plants and even the geology of the district.

Jim and I sometimes worked as game carriers to a party from Manchester who had the shooting at Hearthstane. They only drove grouse once or twice in the season and 'walked up' most of the time, sometimes on the grassier hills of Menzion and Fruid which they also rented. Here the main quarry was blackcock which abounded on the grassy hills with rushy burnsides and steep rowan-filled gullies.

Halfway up a glen on the Menzion farm there was a shepherd's house with two or three small hayfields enclosed with low stone walls. As there were few sources of building stone on this farm, the low walls were topped with turf sods cut from the tough peaty ground. The growth in the sods continued and these walls were frequently used as roosts by black game. One day when the party found a number of birds sitting on the walls and others grazing behind the dykes, a plan was devised which might give the guns a chance of bagging one or two of these old cocks.

Jim and I, being much smaller than the others, were assigned the tricky task of crawling up the edge of the stream, keeping out of sight, to point well beyond the unsuspecting quarry. We were then to show ourselves so that when the birds took flight they would pass in range of the sportsmen who were positioned behind the first wall.

The manoeuvre was completely successful and 22 great cocks – there were no hens with them – streamed towards the centre of the hidden line. Suddenly, when they were nearly in range, they changed direction and poured over the head of the gun at the end of the line. Nothing happened except a belated bang as the gentleman, a Manchester cotton manufacturer, was so overcome by the sight of the approaching aerial armada that he forgot to move the safety catch of his gun to the firing position. This incident illustrates a characteristic of black game who live segregated, male from female, for much of the year.

I started to fish with bait at a very early age and it soon became an addiction. One of my older brothers was a shepherd at Badlieu, some six miles up the valley from Hearthstane, and here too I was able to fish. I also fished further afield with increasing success, and on these expeditions I encountered different kinds of wildlife from those at Hearthstane. By the time I left the Tweedsmuir school in 1920 I had developed an interest in wildlife which remained with me all my life.

Chapter Three   *The First World War*

The events of the Great War of 1914–18 clouded the main period of
my school life. At first it was little noticed by us children and seemed
to be remote. Soon, however, people were talking about events in
Belgium and the retreat from Mons. The possibility of invasion came
into our thoughts when the local Home Guard was formed. These
men, who included our schoolmaster Mr Yellowlees, often drilled in
the open using shotguns, small bore rifles or whatever type of weapons
could be found.

At Hearthstane we came face to face quite soon with the sadness
and sacrifices which had to be endured. Our employer's eldest son,
Billy Thorburn, was in Canada on a sheep ranch when the call for
volunteers was made. He joined the Canadian Expeditionary Force at
once and arrived at Hearthstane on embarkation leave. We boys admired his uniform and the ease with which he spoke to everyone and
looked forward to the time when he would take over the farm. It
seemed that he had hardly left for France before the news came that
he had been killed in action. The rest of the Thorburn family were
soon involved, with Jamie flying, Robert on the sea and Vincent in
the army.

Alec Brown, the postman whom everyone knew, was killed, and
then thick and fast the households of the glen suffered losses – Menzion,
Fingland, Glenbreck, Kingledores, Bield Cottage and Beech Glade. The
arrival of the long, buff OHMS envelopes in the post came to be
feared. They were delivered by Jamie Lawson the postman (postie)
who drove to Tweedsmuir each day from Broughton Post Office
(where the mail came by train) and his task was often very unpleasant
and sad.

The war affected farm activities. With men away at the war, we
children were recruited to help in many ways. Some sheep, especially
the cheviots, had been fed whole maize from South America, but the
German blockade stopped supplies completely. This loss and severe
winter storms reduced the ability of sheep to nurse their lambs. When
lambing time came, it was not completely covered by the Easter holidays
and the shepherds' sons were allowed to stay away from school to
help their fathers.

Crops suffered from lack of fertiliser. Oats were too short to cut with a binder and much had to be cut by scythe or with the hay mower. The latter required two people on the machine, one driving the horses and the other sitting on an extra seat where, with a special rake, the branches were tipped as they gathered on the frame behind the cutter blade. The extra people needed were not available for this operation so the children came to help. My job was to drive the horses which pulled the mowing machine and the ploughman tilted the oats from the seat fitted next to the cutting bar. Making bands and tying sheaves was, of course, the 'bandster's' job. It was sore on our backs and on the hands and arms, especially if there were thistles among the corn.

Hay time meant helping in many ways but mostly with raking. Using a fork was considered too dangerous for us, though if the hay was too dry and slippery we were sometimes put on top of the hay ricks to build them out to the top. The greatest treat at haytime was the pail of ice-cold water slaked with handfuls of oatmeal and stirred enough to make the meal circulate all through the drink. In the afternoon the maid from the farmhouse would come out with a basket loaded with goodies, and if we boys were helping enough we had shares to ourselves.

Hay time ended for us with building the big 'soo' stack behind the byres. The stack was thatched later and the hay was used in sections cut with a hay knife. The sections were called 'dasses' and this system kept the stack waterproof and standing upright until completely finished.

On the domestic front the enemy's blockade meant that every effort was made to increase production. Gardens were well planted and cultivated and methods of preserving produce were improved. As there was a serious shortage of sugar, fruit and other perishables were stored in airtight containers instead of in the usual jars. Potatoes and turnips were stored in clamps and some types of cabbage could be kept in pits with only the outside leaves wasted.

As the war progressed, bread from the bakers' vans became brownish and heavy. In the country where every housewife baked scones for her family, flour became scarce and difficult to use for cooking. Towards the end of the war a shipment of high-quality Australian flour got through the blockade and found its way to the Borders. Not only did the white flour boost morale but the white sacks in which it was packed were made of fine material and proved most useful for making various garments.

Tweedsmuir Home Guard.

One family at least made tallow candles instead of buying the paraffin wax variety. At that time the main light of the house was usually a paraffin lamp which hung in the kitchen/living room, and candles were used to light the bedrooms in the attic. Mrs Turnbull (she was a Laidlaw) of Quilt Burn had the necessary moulds into which the melted tallow was poured with a piece of string in the middle. Some years provided a great deal of tallow from 'braxies' (sheep that had died of disease) but in other years it could be scarce. These candles were very smelly, especially when they were blown out. This was reduced if one used a candle snuffer which prevented the fumes from escaping. Shears, which often accompanied the snuffer, clipped the ends of the burning string if it became sooted over and smokey.

Living in the country had several advantages. There were rabbits and hares for meat, trout from the burns in summer and salmon in winter. Friends and relations in the towns were very glad of the occasional pair of rabbits sent through the post with simply a tie-on label as direction, or a cut of salmon packed tightly as a parcel without much concealment of its contents. By this time Jim and I were growing and learning to catch rabbits and hares as well as trout and salmon.

The wartime shortages had one unexpected effect on wildlife. White hares had for long abounded on our hills and demand for food now made them a marketable commodity. The price rocketed to 5/– each and travelling vans would collect the heavy loads which were brought

Mr Yellowlees, member of the Home Guard.

down from the hills. Shooting and snaring, however, soon reduced their number, and by the time rationing and shortages ended the white hares were comparatively scarce.

One day during the winter of 1916 Jim and I had been watching at the Hearthstane Bridge when we saw some large grey fish passing upstream. They looked different from the usual fish with great humped backs and red snouts. They lacked the usual red and were so fresh and silvery that their shiny scales reflected the surroundings. As it grew dark they were still passing and we hurried home to tell our parents the exciting news. We expected there would be an immediate foray with torch and leister (pronged spear), but no one seemed to believe us or wanted to know.

We were very disappointed and decided that we, at least, would have a go. We had recently bought between us a small carbide lamp from Ally Smith, the cycle dealer in Biggar. It was a Powell and Hanmer and had cost us 3/9d. We filled it up with carbide and water and set out for the river equipped with the big leister which Jim had brought from its hiding place in the byre. A little way above the bridge we lit our rather feeble lamp and started looking at the edge of the still heavy water. The leister had a clodding (throwing) rope on it and Jim kept hold of it to make sure that, whatever happened, we wouldn't lose the weapon.

Because of the depth of the water fish were running quite near the bank, and soon we saw a massive cock fish. Though the leister was as much as I could handle, we got the fish out and put it safely beyond a fence. When we had three very big fish, all kippers (male fish), we thought it was time to stop. We gathered the fish together where a wall hid us from the main road and started for home along the shadows. We tried carrying the fish with the rope threaded through their gills but they were too heavy and we finished dragging them. Once safely home we put the leister away and laid out our booty in front of the two doors.

With difficulty we got our parents to look outside. When the scolding had subsided, the steel yard was produced to weigh our catch. They were the best three fish I have seen in my whole life: 18lbs, 22lbs and 25lbs. We had one, Jim's family another, and the third was distributed with some going by post to relatives living in town.

One day when Jim and I were playing by the edge of the river a soldier in uniform, wearing a large hat with the brim turned up at one side, crossed the nearby Hearthstane Bridge. To our surprise he turned in towards our cottages. Hurriedly we followed and discovered that he was a member of the New Zealand forces who, as a lad, had started work at Wandel when my father was farm grieve. He was on a short leave and had gone to Wandel only to find we were now at Hearthstane so had taken a train to Broughton and walked from there.

The whole night was passed with exchanges of news and anecdotes. He was an orphan and came to Wandel very poorly clad and provided for. His job was to drive the 'odd horse' but he was so small that the horse disdained his authority and gave him a bad time, even biting at unexpected moments. My father had stepped in and gave 'wee Davie', as he was called, the encouragement and confidence he badly needed. I well remember him telling my father how he had benefited from learning from him how to handle farm tools either right- or left-handed.

Alas, he could only stay one night and when he departed the next day he insisted on leaving a beautiful little heart-shaped pendant made of New Zealand greenstone with an inset of a kiwi made in gold. It was for me to wear on my watch chain when I grew up. It was put in the little drawer in the dresser. Sadly wee Davie did not survive the war. I never had a watch and a chain and the gold kiwi pendant remained a keepsake too sacred to wear.

Mr Thorburn had one of the Scots fir woods cut down to provide much-needed timber for building purposes and for coalmines. The felling and moving was done by a family concern from Ettrick Bridge with temporary living quarters at Quilt Burn and stabling at the Crook Inn. Naturally we boys were much attracted to all aspects of the work: the skilled felling and trimming, hauling the timber downhill for loading on to the 'jankers' (long poles with two wheels) and then on to the railway station for transport by rail.

The branches were often burned, especially if they were in the way of the horses, but great heaps remained. We were allowed to take as many as we liked for firewood. My mother was expert in getting this fuel down to the house. Taking a couple of long, strong branches, she laid them on the ground and built up a load crosswise, leaving the ends of the long branches for handles. Using these as shafts, it was possible to drag quite a load at a time. The physical challenge appealed to us lads and we enjoyed the satisfaction of doing something useful.

Coal was now in great demand for industries involved in war work, and soon the price had doubled to over 10/– a ton. On the farm this

Three members of the Home Guard.

increase caused much consternation as shepherds' wages were only between 16/– and 18/– a week and sometimes less when allowances were given in kind. At 5/– a ton coal was quite economical to use but when the price continued to rise it was decided to go back to using peat, which even then was still in use further up the valley. Above the junction of Fruid and Tweed the peat deposits were still in use mainly because they were on low ground and easily accessible. Beyond that point most of the peat occurred on higher ground much further from the farms and cottages.

The peat tools, rusty and unused for many years, were gathered up from odd corners, wall heads and tool sheds, some still with their shafts attached. These were put in good repair and sharpened. The slypes (sledges) were fettled (put in order) and fitted with the framed sides needed for hauling loads of dried peat. So 'flachters' (a special spade used to pare turf from the ground), 'ritters' (another type of peat spade) and 'tuskars' (an iron instrument with a wooden handle for casting peats) were carried out to the peat hags on the high ground on Glenheurie Rig (Ridge of the Glen of the Junipers) where good peat was found.

Peat-cutting required teamwork, and at least three people were needed to work the face. The top turf was shaved off using the flachter, the ritter cut the outside edges to the full depth of the peat and then

1.1 Westwards from the Dreva Road

1.2 Ratchill Farm, Broughton

1.3 The Stobo Road

1.4 Drumelzier Mill

1.5 Looking towards Tweedsmuir and the Talla Hills

1.6 Tweedsmuir Village

1.7 Tweedsmuir
Bridge

TWEEDSMUIR CHURCH

1.8 Tweedsmuir
Church

the tuskar came into use. The main feature of this tool was the sharp blade set at right angles which cut each peat separate from the next. Each peat was about eight inches across and two inches deep and, according to the depth of the deposit, between 15 and 18 inches long.

The peats were full of water, slippery and very heavy. We boys were given the task of catching the wet slices of peat as they were thrown from the shiny blade of the tuskar. To do this we stood in the wet peat hag and used both forearms to keep the peat slices whole before placing them one on top of another at the side of the trench. We were always barefoot as the bottom of the trench was too wet for boots. The peats were then carried away and laid on the turf in orderly lines to dry.

Our fathers worked out a way of saving time. When they had completed the morning round of their respective hills, instead of coming home for food they met at the peat hags and started working on the peats for at least part of the day. If we boys were not at school, or on Saturdays, we were dispatched with food for the men and remained for the rest of the day carrying out the peats and doubling the output.

Peat digging tools. Mr J Sharpe with his collection.

Peat digging tools.

Sometimes we helped with the rest of the peat work, turning, fitting (setting the turf on edge, two and two, for drying), ricking (stacking) and eventually the sledding.

A sledge (slype) with deep runners, also used in snow for hay, was fitted with sides to hold a fair load of peats. Following an old track, the single horse had little difficulty until it came to the steep slope down to the bottom where the peat could be taken on by cart. Although the slope was traversed in a zigzag line, the laden slype tended to speed up at turns and endanger the horse. To act as a brake a heavy chain, which always hung on the slype, was dropped over the front of the runners. This was most efficient, but once on the level it had to be taken off otherwise the horse could hardly move the load. The whole operation was hard and tiring but there was great satisfaction in seeing the finished product in the hearth on a cold winter night.

All the farms in the valley have old peat roads, mostly too steep for anything but slypes. They usually ran at a slant across the hills to reduce the steepness and avoid the tendency of the slypes to increase speed and go too fast for the horses. When ruts, especially at corners, became too deep, new parallel tracks were made which widened the turns. The route for peat cut on Kingledores and taken to Broughton was on the west side of the land. Part of the road joined a track used when limestone was quarried on Glencotho and burned in the kiln on the Wrae. Ned Robertson of Holmsmill told me that his father showed him where the slypes of peat were unloaded and transferred to carts for the last few miles.

At school we were recruited to gather sphagnum moss to make field dressings. Every Saturday in summer a mixed group of the Minister, about ten children, and sometimes another adult or two, took to the hills. We mostly had tackety boots but the Minister wore clumsy goloshes over his unsuitable footwear. His broad-brimmed black hat luckily had a cord attached which was firmly anchored to his jacket lapel. To our concealed amusement it often attempted aerial manoeuvres to escape its fetters.

There was quite a large amount of sphagnum moss growing on the

Jim Lorimer, killed at the Battle of the Somme.

Hearthstane hills in wet, peaty places and on steep, damp, heathery banks. When accompanying our fathers on the hills and when grouse driving, we saw where the plants grew in reasonable quantities, so there was little difficulty in finding enough to fill the sacks we brought with us. As it grew in wet situations, the plant contained stored moisture, and when it was packed in a sack the water soon oozed through and made it difficult to carry the sacks on our shoulders. Each sack was therefore carried between two people, which meant either taking less or making a second journey. There were two collection points, one at the Manse and the other at Oliver. Here the moss was dried, cleaned and eventually sent off to be processed and made into field dressings for use at the war fronts.

Throughout the war the Red Cross was supported by what was called the 'Penny-a-Week Fund' which was collected and contributed to in exactly that way. Some people gave much more than one penny, and when I took the collecting box to Hearthstane farmhouse I knew it would be much heavier after it was passed round the household.

My brother Jim, who had been hill-draining further north, bought a gramophone one day on his way home through Glasgow. It was a 'Robeyphone' and was packed in two strong cardboard boxes. One contained the dark red horn, about two feet long and extending to a similar diameter, and the other a square oak case about six inches deep with the record plate on top. The winding handle folded flat against the side when not in use.

At first we had only a few records, mostly of Harry Lauder and Scott Skinner, and many neighbours came to hear the musical wonder. When funds were required for Red Cross parcels and comforts for the men in Flanders, the gramophone, with some difficulty, was carried in pieces to the village hall where the audience heard music and songs for the first time without the presence of the performers.

Although the horrors of the war and the hardships endured in the trenches were constantly in everyone's mind, there were many happy interludes. We all sang 'Tipperary', 'Keep the Home Fires Burning', the Harry Lauder songs like 'Keep Right on to the End of the Road' and 'Roaming in the Gloaming' with great gusto. The women got great satisfaction in knitting gloves, socks, scarves and balaclavas for their absent men. They baked shortbread, scones, oatcakes and even miniature clootie dumplings. All these were carefully packed up and sent with cigarettes, sweets and occasionally tinned food to individual soldiers at the front. When the local newspaper had been read it was

The new village hall opened in 1926.

tightly wrapped, addressed (often over the paper itself) and sent off with a green ½d stamp attached.

Other 'events' such as whist drives and dances were held to raise funds. Sometimes the whist drives and dances were combined and everyone helped by giving prizes and making cakes and other eatables. These occasions were held in the hall situated at the junction of the Tweed Road and the New (Talla) Road. It was a wooden structure with a tin roof, left over from the building of the Talla Dam when it had been used as a temporary hospital or sick bay. The wooden floor was much worn and springy but after coating with candle wax made a very good surface for dancing.

As these dances were always held on a Saturday night and had to end at midnight, we youngsters were allowed to take part. It was here that we learnt how to dance, not only simple ballroom dances but also the more intricate steps of country dances. Music was supplied by local fiddlers, of whom there was no scarcity, for in nearly every shepherd's house there was a fiddle hanging on the wall in its green or red baize bag.

The dancers did not sit with their partners but on opposite sides of the hall on wooden forms so that when a popular dance was called by the MC there was a sudden rush to the lady of one's choice. At a typical dance two fiddlers would be on a platform and sometimes Jimmie Tod would add his concertina. The first half of the dance always included Flowers of Edinburgh, Petronella, and Drops o'Brandy

Unveiling Day of Tweedsmuir War Memorial.

as well as Scots Reels, Highland Schottische, Polkas, Waltzes, Two Steps, the Lancers and Quadrilles.

Refreshments appeared an hour or so before midnight. A clothes basket full of cups came round accompanied by the dispensers of tea, milk and sugar, followed in turn by sandwiches and home-baked cakes and buns. The second half resumed after a song or two and again included the Lancers and a Quadrille but now in jig time. Sometimes the eatables provided were over sufficient and a second night was arranged.

After the war a new hall was planned with more amenities on another site. Mr Masterton gave a plot of land on the road below the Bield and the new hall was built in 1926. In spite of its better facilities many old-timers still looked back with nostalgia to dances in the Old Hall.

By this time my brother Jim had joined the Scots Guards, a regiment so depleted that most of the new recruits had to be found south of the Border. After much intensive training it was fairly evident that the regiment was intended for what was spoken of as 'the great push' and Jim came home on a short leave. He brought with him two 'double' records. The first had 'Roses of Picardy' on one side and 'Genevieve' on the other. The second was entirely different with Mendelssohn's 'Spring Song' and Schubert's 'Serenade'.

Avoiding going out to meet former acquaintances, Jim spent much of his time playing his favourite records over and over again and holding long, quiet conversations with my mother, which I was not allowed to share. Looking back, it was evident that he did not expect to return from France, a premonition that proved only too true, and he did not survive the bloody battlefield slaughter of the Somme. Somehow the gramophone lost its appeal as it evoked too many memories and after Jim's death was not brought out so often.

The war was making more demands and the Kitchener poster reminded everyone 'Your Country Needs You'. Three of my sisters left to make munitions at the newly constructed factories at Gretna. The work was hard and involved some risk. They had to wear drab trousered overalls and close-fitting caps to keep their hair out of the machinery. Another of my sisters chose to train in dairy work at the agricultural school near Kilmarnock.

The war even affected our play, and pictures of soldiers in dugouts inspired us to try and make a dugout of our own. The site we chose was a dry wooded bank overlooking the river near Hearthstane farmhouse. It was a strategic position which, while hidden, commanded a view across the river and over a mile of the main Moffat road up the valley. At that time there were plenty of worn-out shovels lying around. It had been a rule among the navvies digging the cuttings for the Talla railway that their diamond-shaped shovels should be discarded when worn halfway down. These half-worn but still useable shovels could be found almost anywhere.

We started digging among loose gravel near the mouth of a large rabbit burrow. As we dug down we encountered a network of old rabbit tunnels where, to our horror, we found tiny, almost new-born hedgehogs buried underneath the dislodged soil. Most were already dead, having been smothered and died of suffocation. We shouldn't have been so surprised because when we were looking for a suitable site the previous day we had found the hedgehog family in a tree root, but had put them back safely with their mother.

Thinking perhaps one at least could be saved, I took it home and my mother humoured me by letting me keep it in a box near the fire. It was pink and its eyes were not quite open. It was covered with nodules which would gradually develop into soft spines which would increase in number as it grew. My friends loved to see the strange 'beastie' which I fed regularly with a fountain pen. Just when he had learnt to drink from a saucer he suddenly died. I think that if I had given him cod-liver-oil instead of so much cow's milk he might have survived.

But to return to the dugout. After we had dug a considerable hole, the spoil built up round about and we thought it was time to make a roof. There were plenty of branches nearby to form quite a strong roof under which we could remain concealed and could still see the road well down below the Crook Inn. I don't think we really expected to see the spiked helmets and grey uniforms of the enemy marching towards Tweedsmuir where, of course, the Home Guard would be waiting to ambush them. But sometimes we did manage to spot the water bailiffs on their bicycles and knew to keep off the river and the burn until they were on their way back to Broughton. Long afterwards we could still make out where the Hearthstane dugout kids monitored any unfriendly activity on the road to Moffat.

The end of the war coincided with another devastation as the flu epidemic came to Tweedsmuir and took a heavy toll among young and old alike. The dreaded disease was brought into the glen by a man who had gone to the funeral of a relative near Glasgow. He himself was the first victim, followed by another half-dozen deaths in quick succession. Though some of my family were very ill, we all survived. Soon my sisters were back from their war work and met again their soldier sweethearts. There followed quite a spate of family weddings and the newly married couples settled in the vicinity of Peebles where the farms of Eshiels and Soonhope had been broken up into small holdings for returned servicemen.

The war years, with the losses suffered by nearly all the families in the glen and the needs of the war effort, left us children a more sober or perhaps even a more sombre age group. For example few of us became smokers and most remained teetotal. The austerities of those years were not a complete loss.

Chapter Four   *The Upper Tweed Valley*

I left Tweedsmuir school in August 1920 when I was 14 and the following term became its first pupil to go on to Peebles High school, some 20 miles away. Instead of a mile and a half walk to school each day I now had to cycle six miles to Broughton and take the train to Peebles. After school I had the journey in reverse, which in bad weather was quite a challenge. I became familiar with every bit of the winding road with its steep inclines and welcome downhill stretches.

The road between Tweedsmuir and Broughton is on the west side of the valley and follows the Tweed for most of its way. The track of the railway line, which had been built from Broughton when the Talla dam and reservoir were constructed at the turn of the century, is visible first on one side of the road and then the other, as are the various sheep crossings and tunnels beneath the road. Farms with their stone walls, buildings and cottages can be seen on either side of the river near the burns which feed the Tweed throughout its course.

Once through Broughton, my journey home took me through the parishes of Kilbucho, Glenholm, Drumelzier and then Tweedsmuir. Over the years I became familiar not only with the various landmarks but with the geology of the Upper Tweed Valley and its history. The landscape had been shaped during the ice ages and the configuration of the valley and the surrounding hills with their rugged crags is typical of glacial erosion. In its lower reaches before Broughton the valley is flat enough for fields on either side of the river, but these become fewer in number the further upstream one goes.

Mossfennan, in the parish of Glenholm, was the first estate in the Upper Tweed Valley which I came to on my way home from school. The lodge, which my grandfather had occupied years before, is the only building visible from the road. Little did I know in 1920 that years later I would be the tenant farming the land and living in the large house which I and my wife ran as a guest house.

Mossfennan is mentioned early in the thirteenth century as Mospen-noc when William Purveys gave the monks of Melrose a right of way across his lands to reach their lands of Hopecarton on the other side of the Tweed. By the middle of the eighteenth century several different families had owned the property before it was acquired by Robert

Mossfennan House.

Welsh, whose descendants are in possession to this day. At the time of the Disruption of the Church of Scotland in 1843 Mossfennan was owned by another Robert Welsh, and his nephew, the Revd William Welsh DD, became the first minister of Broughton Free Kirk the same year. In 1855 Dr Welsh inherited Mossfennan from his uncle, and it was during his time that my grandfather was employed by him and lived at the newly built lodge.

Like Stanhope and Kingledores nearby, Mossfennan has several interesting archaeological features including the remains of ancient settlements, cultivation and platform dwellings. These last were situated well up the slopes on the sides of the glens. They were either round or oval in shape, with levelled foundations and without walls. It is not known what the structures themselves were like. Sometimes evidence of fire still remains but no artefacts have been found.

The main house at Mossfennan is over 500 years old in parts and a channel running underneath the building once carried a considerable flow of water with the double function of supplying fresh water and carrying away waste. The property seems to have been well known in the Stuart period, and in one old poem the King of the time was evidently a visitor at Mossfennan 'yett a little alow (below) the Logan Lea'. Another poem from the early eighteenth century concerning the heiress to Mossfennan mentions 'the bob-tailed yous (ewes) that trinkle (trickle) along the Logan Lea'.

The land called Logan adjoins Mossfennan on the south and was part of the Mossfennan estate acquired by the Welsh family. The name in Gaelic means 'little hollow' and is quite common both in the highlands and lowlands. In this instance it is a most accurate description of the site, which was inhabited from earliest times. Unfortunately erosion and damage have taken their toll of the archaeological evidence.

The remains of a fort have almost disappeared. It was built in an almost perfect natural position for defence in times of danger and for protecting the occupants of the dwellings within its walls and also those nearby. The stones were probably incorporated over the years in houses and used for building walls. The dwellings of the early settlement later became a sheepfold. The encircling wall is only traceable by remaining rubble but originally it must have been a sizeable structure. Part of a central building seems to be covered in rubble and might reward excavation.

In recent times when the tunnel was made through the hill to carry water from Talla to Edinburgh, a syphon system was made at Logan with an aqueduct bridge across the glen and into the Wormald. The spill from the tunnel was spread out and on one side covered old terracing and on the other filled up the course of the stream from the settlement water supply to the burn. Pipes were laid underneath the layer of material to carry the water to the burn. Hints of a platform settlement have disappeared with the cultivation of the Logan field and the remains of earlier times are only noticeable now with difficulty on the less ploughable land in dry summers or in times of snow marking in winter.

Once past Mossfennan, my journey back to Tweedsmuir took me into the parish of Drumelzier. On the opposite (east) side of the Tweed Stanhope came into view with its main house and cluster of cottages built near the Stanhope Burn. The name, which comes from the old English 'Stane hope' meaning the Glen of Stones, is an accurate description of the long, deep glaciated glen which joins the Tweed valley.

This large farm was among the possessions of the Murray family from the early seventeenth century. David Murray, son of the first owner, was knighted by Charles I. His son William, who succeeded him, was also a royalist. He suffered greatly under Cromwell, was imprisoned and fined £2,000. Upon the restoration he was created a baronet for his loyalty. Some 80 years later Sir David Murray, the 4th baronet, took part in the rebellion of 1745, was captured and was sentenced to death. His pardon was conditional upon leaving the country and he died in exile. His estates, however, were forfeited and in 1767 Stanhope was sold to Mr James Montgomery, whose descendants owned the property until 1926 when it was sold to Mr Graham Cox.

Prehistoric remains near the present houses and others high up the rocky slopes facing the Tweed, known as Norman's Castle, are of great archaeological interest. Excavations produced signs that weapons or tools had been ground or sharpened there, but a bronze buckle was the only metal object found. These ancient sites have been described in recent archaeological surveys.

At the beginning of the twentieth century the farmer, William Lindsay, quite by chance made a most exciting discovery. He was shooting rabbits on the east side of Stanhope when his dog, while in pursuit of a rabbit, scraped out some copper objects from beneath a large boulder. Upon investigation further objects were discovered including horse furnishings and items of human wear. This Stanhope Treasure, as it was later called, can be seen in the National Museums in Edinburgh.

In more recent times, in the 1920s and 1930s, the *Southern Reporter* ran a regular column of news and comment on country matters written under the pen name Hill Herd. The author was John Dickson, a shepherd at Stanhope. His interesting comments and pawky humour were much appreciated by readers. He was also an accomplished poet, and a collection of his poems was published in 1938. There were many poems of local interest including one on the 'Auld Mill Wheel' at Stanhope. These water-driven wheels, used to grind corn, were once a common and important feature in our rural scene.

Polmood, *c.* 1910.

Going further up the valley, in the wall of one of the Stanhope fields near Patervan farm, there is an inscribed stone marking the site of Linkumdoddie, the supposed home of the subject of Burns's lampoon 'Willie Wastle'. This site was well illustrated in 'The Scott Originals' by the Revd WS Crockett DD, Minister of Tweedsmuir in the early 1900s, except that a lone tree in his picture has long since gone.

Patervan, like Stanhope which it adjoins on the north, is on the east side of the River Tweed. The farmhouse and buildings are close to the Patervan Burn. This farm was part of Polmood until 1965 when it was bought by the Forestry Commission. Since then most of the higher parts have been planted with trees and there have been several changes in ownership. The main house of the old Polmood estate is about a mile and a half further up the valley.

Polmood is of ancient origin and locally was always known as Powmuid. This name is an example of the rich inheritance of place names that has been bequeathed to us, faithfully passed down by word of mouth probably from times long before these names were ever written. They tell us that these wild glens were inhabited at different times by Gaelic speakers, by others who spoke another Celtic language like Welsh, and last of all by those who spoke old Anglo-Saxon from which comes our Scottish Lallans of yesteryear which is now almost extinct.

The name Powmuid is of Gaelic origin. The first syllable means a burn or the glen it passes through and the second is an adaptation of the Gaelic for a hound or for the abode of hounds. Polmood seems to have been associated with the earliest Scottish kings who hunted in these forested glens, and it continued as a royal hunting seat until the end of the Stuart dynasty. In the eleventh century Malcom Canmore entrusted the lands of Polmood to Norman his hunter, but hunting could have been carried on there even earlier if the story of Bonnie Bertha of Badlieu is accepted.*

The royal hunting circuit started at Polmood, and when that hunt

---

* The story of Bonny Bertha refers to a time in the mid-ninth century when Kenneth was king and hunted from Polmood. At Badlieu, further up the valley, a beautiful young girl called Bertha lived with her father. One day the King got lost in the mist while hunting and came to Badlieu where the lovely Bertha caught his eye. He fell in love with her but could not make her his wife as he was already married. He continued to see her and had a son by her despite his wife's jealousy. When he returned from fighting the Danes, he found his wife had died. He immediately went to Badlieu only to find that the jealous Queen, in his absence, had ordered Bonny Bertha, her son and father to be killed.

was over the royal party crossed the hills into Meggat where they stayed at Cramalt. Their route, which is now little known and difficult to trace, followed the Polmood burn until rocky ground made it advisable to move to higher and smoother conditions on the ridge leading to Cramalt. The track uphill to the better ground is well marked but the line following the hard top is visible only here and there.

In the fifteenth century Polmood was part of the Barony of Oliver Castle which was then held by the Frasers and later by the Flemings and then the Hays. The Hunter family remained at Polmood until the nineteenth century. Their crest appropriately included an arm holding a bow and arrow and three hunting horns, with the motto 'Fortuna Sequator'. A descendant, Robert Hunter, married Veronica Murray, daughter of Sir David Murray of Stanhope. She was the half-sister of John Murray of Broughton who was captured at Polmood when he sought sanctuary there after the Battle of Culloden in 1746.

In legal circles Polmood is famous for one of the longest-running actions ever known in the Scottish courts. After 40 years of litigation over the ownership of the estate, Adam Hunter lost his claim, first begun in 1780 against Alexander Hunter and continued against Lady Forbes. In 1847 the estate was sold to Houston Mitchell of New South Wales, Australia. By this time the early seventeenth-century house was in ruins and the present house was built on the site.

As a boy, it was John Hunter whom I knew most about, as it was the epitaph on his grave in Tweedsmuir church that we children had to recite when the Minister visited the school. John Hunter of Polmood was born in 1660 and as a young man was a well-known Covenanter and therefore a wanted man. He had successfully evaded all attempts to capture him at Polmood but met his death in 1685 when he was 'cruelly murdered' at the Devil's Beef Tub by Col. James Douglas and his men.

This story was all the more real to me as on a long ridge known as the Crooked Bank on the side of the Polmood burn there used to be three man-made circular pits known as Hunter's Holes. Their origin was ascribed to the time when hiding places were made for the Covenanters who found precarious safety in these lonely hills. Around 1920 these three holes were still visible and when Jim and I, as inquisitive children, dug into one of them, we imagined we were Covenanters hiding there in the killing times.

These holes were strategically situated in hollows near the top of the ridge with a good view of the area. Each had a hidden escape route into the safety of Glenheurie. Access to these cleverly sited recesses could be gained by a steep gully which would have provided conceal-ment to any fugitive in a hurry. James Hogg must have known about these hiding places, for where he conceals young Carmichael in 'The Bridal of Polmood' corresponds closely with the Hunter's Holes. They must originally have been about 12 to 15 feet across and some 6 or 7 feet deep. Two were situated in peaty ground, and by 1920 the soft sides had crumbled and the growth on the surface had begun to close in. The third pit was dug in hard, dry ground and it remained almost unchanged except that the sides had fallen in. The area now has a forestry road running along it. Crawlers, tractors and bulldozers have hastened the work of time and even the best-preserved pit is largely filled with spill from the forestry road.

Kingledores.

On the west side of the Tweed, opposite Patervan and Polmood and adjoining Mossfennan on the north, is the large farm of Kingledores. The main house and buildings, near the Kingledores Burn, are not easily seen from the road. Like Mossfennan, Stanhope and Polmood, its history can be traced back over several hundred years.

In the thirteenth century, as part of the Barony of Oliver Castle, the property belonged to the Frasers. Early in the fourteenth century the land was divided between the Hays and the Flemings, the Hays owning the land to the north of the burn called Craig Kingledores and the Flemings that to the south. This southern portion was divided into two sections: Chapel Kingledores at the lower part and Kingledores Hope further up the burn.

Chapel Kingledores was named after the thirteenth-century chapel which was built there and dedicated to St Cuthbert. It was on land given by Sir Simon Fraser to the monks of Melrose who also owned Hopecarton across the river opposite Mossfennan. Over the centuries these lands had several owners and tenants and it was not until the early eighteenth century that the whole property came under the owner-ship of one family, the Hays of Drumelzier. In the following century the property changed hands several times, and by the time I started cycling to Broughton each day, it was owned by the Stuart family.

Once past Polmood, I was in the parish of Tweedsmuir. Until 1643 this was all part of the parish of Drumelzier, and the area which was to become Tweedsmuir was known as Upper Drumelzier. The Polmood burn not only forms the boundary between the parishes of Drumelzier and Tweedsmuir, but is also the boundary between Polmood and Hearthstane, the farm to which my family had moved in 1910.

Like Kingledores and Polmood, the land at one time was part of the Barony of Oliver Castle. In the sixteenth century the Hays were the owners and during the eighteenth and part of the nineteenth centuries it belonged to the Tweedies. By the time my family came to Hearth-stane, Mr Thorburn was the owner and the property remained in that family until purchased by the Forestry Commission in the 1960s. Since then the higher parts have been planted and sold and the main house and farm have also changed hands.

The name Hearthstane came into use by mistake through an error made by the first Ordnance Survey. The original name 'Harstanes' indicates boundary stones or rocks which have been removed to fa-cilitate cultivation. One such boulder was blasted by gunpowder just before the 1914–18 war. Evidently the boundary between Hearthstane

The Crook Inn before alterations in 1936.

and Polmood is of comparatively recent date as a dwelling called the Bower of Polmood was originally within the limits of Hearthstane farm.

My family had moved from the cottage at Hearthstane in 1918 and now lived at Glenriskie which was still part of the farm but about a mile further up the valley. This extended my journey home considerably and meant continuing along the road past the old Crook Inn. In 1920 the Inn was still part of Crook farm which had recently been sold to the Masterton brothers of Broughton, but the following year it was sold separately to Mr John Cameron whose daughter, Barbara, was to become my wife some 14 years later.

The road took me past the Crookhaugh Cottages, Glenveg and the Bield, which at one time had been an old coaching inn. Next came the entrance to Oliver, an imposing house higher up and away from the road. I then turned into the lane by the old village hall and over the Tweedsmuir bridge, past my old school and the church and into the lane down to Glenriskie.

The church, manse, school and nearby cottages form the centre of this parish of widely scattered farms and dwellings. The church was built in 1874 on a knoll, probably of glacial origin, which was the site of the former church built in 1648, five years after the parish of Tweedsmuir was disjoined from Drumelzier. Overlooking it all is Oliver, high on the hill on the west side of the Tweed. This eighteenth-

The Bield, *c.* 1910.

century house was built on or near the site of two earlier houses and
not far from the ruins of Oliver Castle. The land was part of the
Barony of Oliver Castle and in the twelfth century belonged to the
Fraser family. It is believed that Oliver Fraser, who built the castle,
granted the land to the Knights Templar who held it until the sup-
pression of their order in 1312. The Tweedie family have been
associated with Oliver since the sixteenth century and the house is
now owned by their descendants, the Tweedie-Stodarts.

When not at school, most of my time was spent on the farm at
Hearthstane or exploring the more remote parts of the Upper Tweed
Valley, far away from the route I took to Broughton. This is a unique
corner of Scotland's Southern Uplands, wild and remote, with deep
glens and tumbling burns, enclosed by a semi-circle of the higher hills
of Dollar Law, Broad Law (Braid Law), Loch Craig Head, White
Coomb and Hart Fell. The area attracts heavy rainfall.

Talla and Fruid, both on the east side of the valley, are the two
main tributaries of the Tweed. Talla joins the river just north of the
church and Fruid joins it to the south of the Tweedsmuir bridge. Where
these burns leave the hills were areas of marshland known as the Talla
and Fruid Lakes. They probably began their post-glacial life as shallow

lochs which later filled up with deposits brought down from the hills. These Lakes acted as sponges and held back the water, so floods were not so sudden as in other parts of the valley.

The high rainfall and numerous strong-flowing burns provide a steady all-the-year-round supply of water, and this has indirectly led to changes in the whole character of the river. In 1897 land at Talla was sold to the Edinburgh and District Water Trustees for the construction of a dam and reservoir to supply water to Edinburgh. A temporary railway line was constructed between Talla and Broughton to bring supplies to the site, and in 1905, five years before my family moved to Hearthstane, the work was completed. Some 60 years later another reservoir and dam were built at Fruid and thus the Lakes disappeared. At the same time large tracts of land, mainly on the hills on the east side of the valley, were planted with trees. High rainfall not only feeds reservoirs but also provides good conditions for forestry plantations.

The name Talla derived from 'Talard' meaning 'the high browed' is found in Wales with exactly the same spelling and accurately describes the nearby hills. The main features of Talla are the tumbling waterfalls known as the Linns and, before the construction of the reservoir, the Lakes. The whole area abounds with interest with names like Carlareen (Welsh), Garelet (Gaelic) and Gameshope (Old English). The smaller narrow glens are 'cleuchs'. One of these called Donald's Cleuch is said to be named after Donald Cargill, a famous covenanting divine who preached at a large conventicle held there in 1681 shortly before he was captured and executed.

The expressiveness of our native dialect is exemplified in the name 'the Cherkin' or 'Cherkin Bog' which aptly describes a few acres of rushy bog land high up on the shoulder of the Garelet. The expression, though little used today, may renew memories of soaking boots and stockings as well as wet ground and sticky 'glaur' or mire.

Gameshope Burn, which once joined Talla at the foot of Talla Linns near the farm buildings, now flows into the end of the reservoir. Near the source of this burn there is a small loch which must be one of the highest in the country. The whole area round Talla and Gameshope is of geological interest and the rocks and crags have given refuge to eagles, falcons and ravens through the centuries. Historically the Hay family had long connections with Talla and during the troubled times of Mary Stuart one member was caught up in the plotting and violence of the period. He was depicted in a poem of the time as 'wild as the roaring Linn, young Hay of Talla'.

The transformation of the Lakes into the reservoir completely changed Talla. Our knowledge of the area now depends on anecdotes of young shepherds there during a long period when the farm was herded almost entirely by young unmarried men. The accounts of these early, almost legendary times are now second-hand but I, among others, was fortunate enough to hear them from those who had themselves participated in the events they narrated in the true 'Lallans tongue o' the Borders'.

Fruid, derived from the Welsh 'frwyd' meaning impulsive, indicating sudden changes, cannot apply to the actual water flow of this large burn as the Fruid Lakes effectively slowed the floods and retained much of the flood water. Changes, however, are seen in the physical course of this tributary of the Tweed whose source is in a great basin high on Hart Fell. It first wanders slowly among deep peat hags, then suddenly drops some 500 feet in continuous waterfalls, called in the vernacular 'The Spoot Heeds'. In heavy spate the falls all join together to make a single foaming cascade. The burn then continues among glacial boulders and debris until it reaches its last rocky waterfall, the Hawk Linn. The rock around this Linn protects an area of interesting plant life from sheep, and a surprising variety of native plants has survived including trees and bushes which have grown from seeds brought by birds roosting in the original rowan trees.

After it is joined by Ellerscleuch Burn, named after the sauchs (willows)

Oliver.

The road to Tweedsmuir Bridge.

called 'ellers' or 'allers' which grow among the boulders, Fruid becomes a gravelly stream for some two miles before entering what is now a reservoir but was previously the Lakes. Here it meandered lost among pools, bushes, bogs and tall rank vegetation. Below the reservoir more gravelly streams and a series of waterfalls bring Fruid to its confluence with the Tweed above what was once a useful ford called Fruid Foot Ford.

Historically Fruid was long associated with the Frasers who were granted the lands by David I. Nothing remains of the castle which a member of that family built at Fruid before Oliver Castle was built in the main Tweed valley. Various names in the area recall its history. Among these is Strawberry Hill which is a reminder of the Fraser family whose emblem was a strawberry leaf. The name Priesthope is all that remains of the small chapel near Carterhope. The Reevers Road, now hardly traceable, which crosses from the head of the Annan to Carterhope, recalls much earlier times.

Menzion Burn flows between Talla and Fruid and is not only much smaller but its course is less dramatic. Like the other two, its name has survived almost unaltered from its original form, Mynyn, meaning a mossy moorland – an apt description before afforestation. Originally part of the Barony of Oliver Castle, the history of Menzion follows closely that of Gameshope. Upon the death of Sir Simon Fraser these lands were divided between his daughters who had married into the

Tweedsmuir Church.

Tweedsmuir Manse, *c.* 1910.

Fleming and Hay families. Eventually in the seventeenth century they became the property of Sir David Murray of Stanhope. Talla and adjoining land at Hearthstane was inherited by the Hay family and, like Fruid and Menzion, later changed hands several times and large tracts became forestry plantations.

Near Menzion house, on the road leading from Tweedsmuir to Menzion, can be seen an arrangement of upright stones known locally as the Giant's Stones. In early maps these are recorded as a Druid's Circle. Though only three stones stand there now, it seems very likely that at least some of the others have disappeared and perhaps were used when the road was made through the middle of the circle. At the highest point of the circle a slightly raised area when ploughed showed that a section had been floored with selected stones of similar size all fitted together. Some sections of this flooring remained intact in the giant furrows though turned upside down. Certainly long ago someone must have arranged and upended these stones with much effort for a particular purpose. Unfortunately it was all too easy for modern machinery to spoil this site and ruin an ancient archaeological feature.

Between Fruid and its source, some seven miles further south, the Tweed, now smaller, meanders through an area, wild and bleak, with little arable land. The farms are few and far between and much of the hill land has become forestry plantations. Hawkshaw and Fingland, the next two hill farms beyond Fruid on the east side of the Tweed, were connected with the Lindsay family, ancestors of the Earls of Crawford, and the Porteous family for several centuries. Early maps show that there was once a tower near the Hawkshaw Burn. Since then these lands have had several different owners. On the opposite side of the river, Glenbreck and the neighbouring lands of Badlieu are believed to have belonged to the Crown before becoming part of the Barony of Drumelzier.

Badlieu was held by the Hunter family of Polmood at one time, as was the adjoining land of Tweedhopefoot. This last farm lies on both sides of the river and extends almost to its source to the east and to the hills dividing the valleys of the Tweed and Clyde to the west. They were bought by Houston Mitchell of Polmood in 1847 and later changed hands several times. In the early part of the twentieth century a small subsidiary school was opened in a tin hut near the road at Tweed-hopefoot for children at this end of the valley and was used for a number of years. Tweedshaws and Earlshaugh, which adjoin Tweed-hopefoot, are the last farms in the valley and include the source of the Tweed and Cor Water, a tributary, which joins the Tweed on its east bank. Both properties were part of the Barony of Drumelzier. Tweed-shaws farmhouse, which is by the roadside, was once an inn.

The name Badlieu comes from the Gaelic 'Bad Laogh' meaning thicket of the calf or calving. The thickets would almost certainly have been saugh (willow) which under natural conditions spreads outwards while the older and taller growth in the middle matures and eventually

The road to Glenriskie.

dies. Cows in the wild seek a safe hiding place when calving so the calves can be concealed while the dam forages nearby. The clumps of saughs would be ideal and would probably be used year after year. Another site nearby is called Badenteric meaning the thicket of the bull. As the hunting ground of the earliest Scottish kings, operating most likely from Polmood, one gets the impression that the quarry might have been the wild cattle as well as deer. The tragic story of Bonnie Bertha and Kenneth, her royal lover, still haunts Badlieu.

About a mile up Badlieu Burn a tributary called Polskene is known by old herding families as Powskene, the burn of the bushes. I remember a stell (shelter) there with sheep buchts (folds) and a small stone-built kebhouse (building used for ewes and abandoned lambs) which at one time must have been an inhabited dwelling. Around the ruins were signs of enclosures made with sods. It was here that a group of fugitives from the Battle of Rullion Green in 1666 made a fire to cook a stirk (bullock) lifted or bought from Hawkshaw. At first light all had vanished across the hills toward their distant Galloway homes. Forestry ploughs and smothering pines have now permanently hidden whatever may have remained of the dwelling.

A Roman road from the Solway to the Clyde skirted the south-western watershed for several miles. Remains of forts at Chester Lees and Chester Knowes, all on the east side of the Tweed, chart the progress of the Romans down the valley. In medieval times a road followed

Talla Water Works – opening day, 1905.

the valley southward on the west side of the river into Annandale towards Carlisle and the English borders. Its course can be traced much further away from the river than the present route, mainly to avoid floods and boggy ground.

In early times, owing to the difficulty of fording the Tweed, another track on the east bank could be used and was still the main route for livestock until the coming of motor transport. Drove roads crossed the district through passes in the hills. In places the tracks were cut out by hand and well-made sections can still be seen. One such section cuts across from Glenholm to Kingledores Hopehead where it divides. One branch goes towards Tweedsmuir and another, clearly marked in places, followed the upper edge of Green Syke into Oliver and Glenbreck toward the main valley. Another led through Mossfennan nick and was still in use in the early years of the twentieth century for stock going to markets in Lanarkshire.

According to tradition the Reevers Road, from Annan Water to Carterhope and Fruid, was one of the routes used after cross-border raids to distribute cattle from south of the Border which had been hidden in the Devil's Beef Tub. In good conditions the road could take wheeled vehicles and in the mid-eighteenth century was used by a local Moffat farmer who also farmed in Fruid. Empty carts could follow this route to Fruid but, when laden with wool, returned by the alternative route over Fruid Foot Ford to the main road.

Talla, Fruid and all the other farms on the east side of the river depend on bridges for access. The Tweedsmuir Bridge, known locally as the Linn Brig or Carlowes Brig, was constructed in 1783, almost 150 years after Tweedsmuir became a parish in its own right. The narrow gorge of solid bedrock, below two falls, was the most suitable place for the bridge to be built. The name, like so many Celtic names, describes the features. 'Car' or 'Caer' refers to the rock, 'Lowes' to the pouring water and 'Linn' to the pool. Thus this is the bridge over the pool of the rock of pouring water. When one looks over the upper parapet one can see both falls.

At the beginning of the twentieth century the water of the lower fall dropped several feet in a solid spout into a foaming whirlpool. Generations of children, myself included, spent much time watching with fascination the efforts of fish of all sorts and sizes literally throwing themselves at the column of falling water. The water of the upper fall dropped into the main gorge beside a tall spike of rock, some 8 or 10 feet high, and in very high floods it stood in the middle of a foaming cascade. Below the bridge on one side of the Linn, a smooth wall of solid perpendicular rock rises 10 feet or more above the river level. This end of the Linn provides a haunt for pied wagtails which feed on the flies which hatch on the rocks.

In late winter or early spring, after a prolonged period of frost and snow, the river was subjected to large ice floods. These were quite spectacular, especially at Carlowes Brig where they were accompanied

Gameshope.

Glenbreck.

by a great deal of noise. Vast sheets and chunks of ice were tossed over the rocks in the narrow gorge and tore away soil and sods from the field on one side and from the edge of the trees on the other. When the ice had all passed, the rocks were left shining and clean. After one such flood the schoolmaster found an otter which had been crushed to death by lumps of ice. When summer came, the crannies in the rocks sprang into life with thyme, mosses and even harebells which had found footholes there. There was even a small alpine plant whose name I never knew. All had somehow survived the grinding ice and flood waters.

Stanhope, Patervan, Polmood, Hearthstane, Hawkshaw and Fingland all rely on bridges. These were originally made of wood, using strong tree trunks for uprights and heavy planks and stout rails for the other parts. Severe floods after great storms and frosts in 1884 carried away the wooden bridges below the Tweedsmuir Bridge which, as it was stone-built, survived. Much of the timber which was swept down the river was retrieved on the haughs further down the valley at Drumelzier and Dreva. The bridges were rebuilt and some of the old timber was reused. Stanhope, Patervan and Hearthstane bridges were rebuilt with timber but the Polmood Bridge was replaced by one of iron, built by the engineer who had built the Forth Railway Bridge.

The Hearthstane Bridge, like its predecessor, crossed the Tweed at right angles directly onto the main road. It had three spans so, though

The Source of the Tweed.

the ends rested on the banks, it needed two sets of supporting pillars each made of the trunk of a tree. Though quite high above the running water, there were times when floods rose within a few feet of the walkway. One spring in the early 1920s a great deal of ice had formed up Tweed and in the Lakes of Fruid. The break-up came with a sudden thaw and flood. Great sheets of thick ice became jammed, like a log-jam in Canada, lodging on the pillars of the Hearthstane Bridge, and stopped the flow. As great masses of ice built up, blocks were carried over the river bank and onto the main road where they remained until they were carried down towards the Crook. When the ice blockage gave way, it left the upright supports of the bridge torn and damaged and the roads impassable until cleared of piles of ice, mainly in sheets 5 or 6 inches thick. The ice flood had scoured the river banks and had removed bushes growing on the margins of the river. Extensive repairs had to be made to the bridge including protective shields on the upstream faces of the pillars.

Tales abound of the difficulties herds encountered in times of prolonged frosts, heavy snow and floods. The earliest snowstorm in my own lifetime in which I participated occurred in the spring of 1917 after a very hard winter of both frost and snowfall. Lambing had started when a heavy fall of snow accompanied by a high wind piled huge drifts up behind and against the stone walls round the fields. Jim Anderson and I were about eleven years old and we were directed to search for covered ewes and lambs behind the dykes at Hearthstane. As it had been such a bad winter, many sheep were in poor condition and had been brought in to the fields from the hills for protection and better feeding. They had huddled together in the lee of the walls for shelter only to be covered over in the drifts. The snow, however, was light and powdery and we managed to get some out quite easily. In most cases we had to poke into the snow with sticks to locate the buried animals and then dig them out.

Lambing had already started and, surprisingly, most of the lambs were alive and lying under their mothers who had stood over them all the time. Among the dead most were cheviots which were not so well clad with wool as the blackfaced sheep. Our fathers were away to their hills where conditions were dreadful. The weather changed for the better but too late, and a poor lambing average came when the country badly needed food owing to the war shortages.

On Badlieu that year a number of sheep had been buried in a cleuch (narrow glen) where there were peat hags with overhanging edges. Most of the sheep were dug out safely but the extreme frost hardened the snow, and those unaccounted for were given up. Weeks later two or three came out from a place where the hags had kept the snow from bearing down on them and eventually only one remained to be found and found she was, 49 days after the storm. She had been under the overhang of a hag and had eaten all the wool she could reach off her flanks right down to the skin. Some of the overhanging roof of her prison contained roots of grass and heather and these had helped to keep her alive. She was carried home weak and emaciated but recovered in the shelter of the hay shed with special nourishment of kiers (treacle and water), though she remained a strange-looking object with a ruff of wool round her neck and bare right down to her hindquarters.

For all its beauty, the Upper Tweed Valley was a very hard place in which to live and work, particularly in the days before electricity, telephones and motorised transport. Life, particularly in winter, was an enormous challenge both to man and beast. There have been many changes in my lifetime. Large tracts of hill land have been planted with trees, fewer people are employed on the farms and more gain their living elsewhere. In 1960 the parish became linked with Stobo and Drumelzier and no longer has its own Minister resident in the Manse. In 1978 the school closed and children now attend the school at Broughton. It is very different to the time when I first cycled to Broughton to catch the train to Peebles in 1920.

Chapter Five *Farming*

I grew up in a community consisting almost entirely of shepherds whose lives were devoted to the care of over 20,000 sheep covering an area of some 40,000 acres. Altogether there were 27 married shepherds with their families and about 13 young unmarried herds. Taking the area in 'waters', the term for large glens, Talla had only two married shepherds but usually three or four young unmarried herds; Fruid and Menzion had seven married and four unmarried; Up Tweed also had seven married and four unmarried; Down Tweed had 11 married and only one unmarried herd, although farms with arable land took on young men for summer work. This situation remained almost unchanged until the Second World War, after which there were great changes in the ownership and use of the land.

Before the 1914–18 war Hearthstane Farm extended to the river Tweed on the west for about two miles between Polmood and Talla. Polmood Burn formed the northern boundary and Talla the southern. The longer eastern boundary mainly followed the watershed of the Talla and Megget rivers and included most of Broadlaw. The glen of the Hearthstane Burn, with its main tributary Glenheurie, stretched some four or five miles through the middle of the farm with Glenriskie and Motte burns flowing into the Tweed.

Five men were employed on the farm: three married shepherds to look after some 2,000 sheep, a young shepherd who also acted as a ploughman, and a cattleman-cum-gardener. At lambing time each of the married shepherds had help for three weeks from lambing men, and at clipping time extra help was needed for tying the wool.

Several farms in the district worked on a similar system because of their physical structure and size. At this time a herding covered about 1,000 to 2,000 acres grazing 500 to 1,000 lambing ewes with over 100 young age ewes to replace the 100 or so old ewes culled each autumn. The hogs (1st year) were not put in lamb until they became gimmers (2nd year) and were usually sent to lower farms for their first winter. Dairy farms in Ayrshire and Lanarkshire regularly took wintering hogs.

Drumelzier Castle.

Animals from the same farms were wintered year after year for a fixed payment for each surviving sheep.

This period, November 1st until April 1st, was supposed to increase the size and improve the later performance of the animals. Cast ewes (six-year-olds) were apt to have broken mouths (missing teeth) but throve well on lower ground farms and produced a good crop of lambs with many twins. These lambs were usually crosses (Border/Leicester) and grew and fattened quickly.

The shepherd's year coincided with the breeding cycle of sheep, from 'tup time', November 22, onwards. Tup time, with free running sheep on open hefts (unfenced ground) was a test of a shepherd's skill. The tup (ram) for each heft had to be unrelated to the ewes and, especially if he had been used on an adjacent heft, could never be allowed to stray from his own woolly harem. Daily counting of the sheep became necessary at this time. Weather affected the animals, and sometimes snow on the high ground could be an advantage by keeping the sheep from straying away from their home territory.

The shepherds were completely dependent on their sheepdogs to work their flocks. Most of these dogs were well looked after and well fed, as the shepherds' 'bargain' (conditions of employment) included an oatmeal ration for their dogs. A minority of herds took their collie dogs very much for granted and treated them carelessly. Occasionally one might meet a herd with several dogs with matted coats, dirty and unkempt. Matts, lumps of hair grown and stuck together, eventually came off, leaving patches of nearly bare skin beneath. When these dogs cast their winter coats it was not a pretty sight.

The Border Collie in the early 1900s was not so uniform as it is today. Some people liked 'beardies', the rough, coarse-haired type akin to the English long-haired with even their eyes almost hidden. They could be mainly grey in colour though the general trend was toward black and white. Usually they were white collared with a white stripe down the front of the face. Although they worked by sight and sound, these dogs still had a strong scenting power.

Other shepherds preferred the medium-coated variety. The short-haired collies, termed 'bare skinned', had one great advantage over the other two: in snow they remained unencumbered by 'balling', the term used when snow gathered and froze on the long hair on legs, tails and bellies. This frozen snow built up, and sometimes the poor animals were completely exhausted and almost unable to move. The frozen lumps had to be cut off with the risk of cutting into the underlying skin. 'Balling' could be reduced if fat was rubbed onto the feathered underparts where snow would gather.

The training of sheepdogs consists of controlling their powerful instincts and using their intelligence and desire to please. Shepherds, of course, varied very much in their approach and power over their canine assistants. Nevertheless the sight of a shepherd operating and controlling a batch of sheep is a sheer delight and thrill even to those who do not understand all the finer points of their training and work.

Hill lambing started in mid-April on most farms and was preceded by 'udder looking' when the whole hirsel was examined. Barren ewes were marked, usually on the rump with a keel mark, and lambing ewes had any surplus wool stripped from round their udders to enable the new-born lambs to have unhindered access to the teats. Those few showing signs of having twins were kept in the fields.

Certain areas of the hills were favoured by the expectant mothers, and some individuals used to lamb far away from their home ground, returning to the same place year after year. These annual journeys, some of several miles, figured in the experiences of the older shepherds from times when fences and walls were less common.

On cold sleety mornings lambs often became too numbed with cold to stand up and drink their mothers' colostrum. If the dam stayed with it and the herd arrived in time, he could save it by catching the

2.1 Cattle at Woodend, Mossfennan

2.2 Sheep by a Woodland Burn

2.3 Herding Sheep at Stanhope

2.4 Hope Carton

2.5 Sheep Clipping at Mossfennan

2.6 Peat Cutting at Glenheurie

2.7 Watering the Team

2.8 View up Glenholm

mother and helping the offspring to suckle. Many, however, had to be carried back to the peat fires where, with massage and warm cow's milk, life often returned to the starving mite. In those days shepherds wore plaids, and lambs were carried tucked in the folded corners. Later, when plaids were less common, the shepherd carried a 'lambing bag' over his shoulder. This was simply the lower part of a hessian sack with a strap over the shoulder which provided more space than the plaid.

While still young, we children were able to take part in all the seasonal activities of sheep husbandry. When more help was needed with lambing, we were allowed to take time off school to help our fathers. This meant rising at first light, which was very difficult initially but proved good training for the future.

We absorbed much of the lore attached to sheep from our parents and neighbours, including two superstitions associated with lambing time. One superstition was that it was unlucky to shave during this period, and the other was that any dead sheep should not be buried until all were lambed. The last probably had some reason behind it since infection could have been carried on the shepherds' hands and passed on to sheep handled later.

In many instances there simply wasn't time to attend to burials, and by the time the intensive work was over the carcasses were too far gone to skin, though it was still possible to remove the the wool by 'sloughing', pronounced 'sluching'. This wool had a most unpleasant odour yet, when it was kept for a week or two in a loose sack, the smell went away or at least became bearable. The fallen wool and 'sluchs' were part of the shepherds' perquisites and were sent to local firms to be processed. The resulting cloth, blankets or knitting yarn were returned to the shepherds' wives.

Many herds knitted stockings for themselves and their families and there were some who were said to be able to keep on knitting while walking round their hills. One shepherd who found it difficult to make ends meet had the fallen wool and that from his 'pack' (the animals he was allowed to keep for himself) made into knitting yarn. He and his wife knitted scores of pairs of socks, and when attending the markets the following year he took a supply with him to sell to his fellow shepherds.

The problem of carrying goods while driving a flock of lambs to market was solved by stringing the socks round his waist underneath his jacket, thus keeping the hosiery dry and at the same time easily available for customers. By the end of the sheep sales he had successfully disposed of his stock-in-trade and made much more money than he could possibly have realised from the raw wool which at the time could hardly be sold even though only a little over a penny per pound.

The idea that it was unlucky to shave during lambing time is more difficult to understand. Some lambing men, apart from the regular shepherds, had come a long way from their homes and brought with them a minimum of luggage. In some instances they slept in fairly rough conditions and had an excuse for not shaving. Perhaps the saving of time at a critical period lay behind the superstition, and the extra few minutes could be used for the benefit of the sheep and their lambs.

As I grew I was encouraged to help with the sheep at dipping and clipping time. Dipping involved a team of three: one to push the sheep into the long narrow dipper, another to momentarily push the sheep below the surface of the dip, and the third to open and shut the the gates controlling the two special pens (dreepers) where the soaking sheep stood while the surplus dip ran off them and back into the dipper.

When the sheep in one of these pens had dried out, the outlet gate was opened until all were gone, then it was shut and the other opened to take the sheep coming straight from the dipper. My job was to keep the drying pens going well with one dreeper alternating with the other. It was a continuous process which enabled the sheep to be sent through without stopping. As long as I kept the drying pens going well, the work continued apace.

While handlings like udder looking, lamb marking and dipping were important, the main sheep handling of the year was the clipping, and for us boys it was the most exciting. The blackface and cheviot sheep kept at Hearthstane Farm were not ready for shearing at the same time, so we had two clippings. Hogs (yearlings) were usually clipped on the same day as the lamb marking, around mid to late June. This wool, especially from the cheviots, was more valuable than that of the later clipping and had to be kept separate.

The main clipping was in late July. Clipping days started very early. As the sheep had to be gathered before they had time to feed, we were usually away to the hill at 3 o'clock in the morning before the arrival of full daylight. The gatherers and their dogs aimed to be at the furthest limits of the ground before the flock had time to eat too much. Handling a sheep with a full stomach for clipping on a stool was difficult and could even prove fatal.

Clipping at Hearthstane.

The shepherds, each with at least two dogs, would go to the highest point of their hirsels and, without hurrying them, gathered their sheep, ewes, lambs, hogs and sometimes even tups, and worked them downhill towards the clipping folds which they would reach at about 5am or 6am. Occasionally some of the flock were brought in the previous day, but most hirsels were gathered on the morning of the great day.

The first operation was to put the flock through the shedder to separate the animals to be clipped from the others. Lambs and hogs (already clipped) were kept back and only the ewes went on to the holding buchts (pens) ready to progress into the gripping pen and eventually to the clipping stools. By this time the shearers were arriving from neighbouring farms and were taking their places on the clipping stools, often in the same order as in previous years.

All shearing until the early 1920s was done on stools, wooden constructions of varying patterns which accommodated both shepherd and sheep. Few farms in Tweedsmuir had enough stools, so they were lent in rota. In the case of Hearthstane a cartload of stools was brought from Menzion the night before and a reciprocal arrangement would follow when Menzion clipped later.

Ground clipping gradually became popular among the younger men as it was faster and did not require the sheep to have their legs tied. The older generation, however, stuck to the stools which in some ways required less bending and allowed a sitting position most of the time.

Horses and men.

Personnel circulated between the farms as well as clipping stools. Hearthstane, Menzion, Patervan and Talla all 'neighboured' – the term used to denote the communal use of manpower and resources. A similar group of farms at the top of Tweed also 'neighboured', and these included Fruid, Badlieu, Glenbreck, Fingland and Hawkshaw.

By 7am most of the shearers had arrived, mostly on bikes, though the older generation walked as they found it difficult to learn to cycle. Balancing on two wheels seemed to them to defeat the laws of gravity and they felt safer on their own two feet. Once assembled, overalls (usually white) were donned, shears, sharpening stone and a small bottle of oil were produced from a bag along with a tying belt or strong thong which was well oiled and soft to avoid cutting into the legs of the tied animals.

Once the shearers were in place on their clipping stools, the 'roughies' (unclipped sheep) were released into the clipping fold in numbers equivalent to the number of clippers. Each sheep was then turned onto its back in front of a clipper and had two of its legs tied together so clipping could begin. As each sheep was clipped, the shearer would call 'roughie' to the catchers who then released another sheep to take its place. Immediately after being clipped but before being released, the sheep were 'buisted' (marked with the identifying initials of the farm) – an operation which I will describe later.

The continuous calls of 'roughie' and 'buist' kept the catchers oper-

Fox shooting at Kingledores, 1917.

ating under considerable pressure. The catchers had a hard task as the sheep had to be caught inside the gripping pen and propelled to the clipping stools. This task became increasingly difficult as the pen emptied, and sometimes a sheep arrived at the clipping stools with a catcher astride its back, or holding its horns or neck. In the case of cheviots a grip on the long wool on the shoulder was employed. Occasionally the catchers resorted to the method of 'bolting' when one catcher inside the pen released a sheep and allowed it to bolt through the open gate to apparent freedom. The other catcher stood outside the gate and gripped the racing ewe as it passed. If more than one ewe escaped at once, the escapees had to be caught later from among the clipped sheep.

All this time the 'tyers' had been busy. Each fleece was gathered as soon as it came from the sheep and carried to a low table where two people, usually women, would roll it up. This was done by one tyer making a rope of the neck by either pulling or cutting the fleece, while the other tyer folded and rolled the body of the fleece from the other side of the table. The twisted rope was then taken in one hand and whipped round and tucked firmly through, like tying a corn sheaf. Blackface fleeces were wrapped with the wool still on the outside while the cheviot fleeces were tied with the inside out, which required a different technique on handling.

The work of the shearers went on apace with few interruptions.

Some even had two pairs of shears so that when one became blunt the other came into use. Carborundum was not then in use for sharpening, and instead hones, sometimes of local stone, were employed with oil to give grip to the face of the shears. Sharpening was quite a skill and the cantle or angle of the cutting edge was varied to suit the kind of wool being sheared. An obtuse angle was a 'short cantle', a fine angle was a 'long cantle' and more used with cheviots. In some parts sharpening was done by dipping a flat stick in grease and then in dry sharp sand. This was done only where the right kind of sand could be found.

After about an hour or more of clipping, breakfast would be provided at a long trestle table. The clipping would then continue until dinnertime at noon. This meal usually consisted of soup, cold mutton and potatoes, with tea and scones to follow. All these meals were provided by the shepherds' wives. The afternoon session always seemed harder, drinks were more in demand and the shears needed 'fettling' (sharpening) more often. At teatime the womenfolk brought food out and a short break was taken on the spot.

As the shorn sheep accumulated in the outer run, there was much bleating both inside and outside the folds as the lambs and their mothers carried out dialogues of recognition. All this time the heap of fleeces rose higher and higher, and packing it into sheets provided by the wool merchants was the last important job of the day. Each sheet, capable of holding between 60 and 70 fleeces, was suspended in turn by strong ropes just clear of the ground on a gibbet – a feature of every sheepfold where clipping was done. There were traditional ways of putting up the ropes and a special method of tying the ropes to the top corners of the sheet. This was done by using a round stone inside the fabric to give a knot that would not slip but could be untied by one jerk on the rope end.

When several fleeces had been packed into the hanging sheet, two of the most agile of the company pulled themselves up by the ropes and the crossbar of the gibbet and the tramping of the wool began. Sometimes children helped by carrying fleeces from the heap but usually only adults handed them up to the trampers. When the sheet was full and evenly packed, metal skewers were used to hold the straining, overlapping edges on the mouth until they could be sewn together. The sack was then removed from the framework and replaced with an empty one. The next stage of the process was to sew up the top of the full sack, starting at the middle and working towards the corners.

This operation was carried out by the older men who used curved needles, string and locking stitches each measuring 4 or 5 inches in length. The corners were then firmly tied, leaving 'ears' as handles, and the string was left hanging to accommodate a tie-on label which gave details of the wool and farm on one side and the destination on the other. If the wool had to be kept, it was loaded onto carts and put in a weatherproof shed as it had to be kept dry.

Towards the end of the day the lambs were released and a lively and noisy scene ensued with much confusion when lambs found it hard to accept their mothers without their fleeces although they recognised the familiar voice. Some lambs would find their way to the heap of fleeces, hoping to find their mothers by smell.

During the more difficult times wool prices were very low and some farms kept their crop until the following year in the hope that the price would rise a penny or so – this was a considerable amount when wool was fetching around 2d per lb. Sheep carried heavier fleeces then and the length (staple) of the wool was nearly twice that of today. Cheviot wool, however, commanded a much higher price than Blackface wool.

The number of people involved in an ordinary farm clipping in those days was very high compared with modern times. The number of clippers usually ranged from nine or ten upwards to nearly twenty, and each could clip between five up to twelve or even fifteen sheep per hour, depending on the condition or 'rise' of the fleece. There would be two catchers, two wool tyers, one or two buisters and someone bringing in the sheep to the catching pen. In addition the womenfolk of the farm were all involved in the catering side. The communal nature of the sheep clippings made each an important social occasion and engendered neighbourliness and good relations – important factors for keeping up the quality of country life.

Tups were clipped early, about the same time as the hogs, and because they were few in number the herds did the job without outside help. It took only an hour or two and Jim and I were allowed to attend. On one occasion when we were very small, no more than 5 or 6 years old, there was a very belligerent old tup, and the young shepherd, as a challenge, had taken on the task of relieving him of his fleece. It was quite a struggle, and after all the others were finished he was released. For a second he stood glaring at the onlookers and, lowering his head, he charged the weakest part of the line which comprised Jim and me. Jim nipped behind my father and I turned to run behind Jim's father but I was too late. The tup's head hit me so low that I was thrown up over his shoulders and rolled down his back. Except for some bruises on my legs I was none the worse but I had acquired a considerable respect for blackface tups and their horns.

Many years later I encountered another blackface tup with strong inborn belligerency. A neighbouring farmer had a comparatively small flock and could only use any tups he bought for two seasons. I heard he was selling a good tup which came of very good stock but I didn't know his reputation for bad temper. When I went to collect him, the shepherd wouldn't go into the pen beside him and warned us to be ready to jump out of his way. I discovered that he would attack any other tup that got in his way and terrified most sheepdogs. He did well and bred good lambs but ruled the roost among the other tups. Some time later the old bully met his Waterloo and his badly battered body was discovered in a hidden corner of the field where the rams were kept after tupping time.

By the end of the nineteenth and the beginning of the twentieth century sheep farming was changing rapidly. Farms tended to become bigger and the use of fencing in addition to the walls already there made the work of the shepherd, if not easier, at least more effective. When open marches (unfenced boundaries) were the rule, the shepherd had to be able to recognise all the sheep in his charge, and the art of 'kenning' was a good herd's trademark. Naturally it was advisable to keep the same herd looking after the same animals both from the employer's as well as the shepherd's point of view, and many families handed on the herding for many generations. One Tweedsmuir family (Renwick) herded the same hirsel for over 300 years.

The effectiveness of the fences which came into general use as boundaries depended a good deal on weather. In severe conditions and heavy snowfall they could sometimes be completely covered, allowing the sheep to cross easily in search of food. If a thaw came, or sometimes a change in wind which moved the snow, the return could be cut off.

Aids to the recognition of sheep came into use with a system of earmarking, horn burning and sawcuts, and even in some cases branding. A special local register was set up to cover these stock marks, especially ear marks, but including keels and 'buists' (identifying marks), all of which were intended to make it easy to prove the ownership of straying sheep. A newspaper column 'Lost and Found' was much in use. A huge number of variations in the marking of ears made it unnecessary for the same mark to be used in farms anywhere near each other.

These registers of stockmarks had some spare pages and spaces which were used for notes and information. Hearthstane's book was kept by Jim's father. One of these books which was used by Jimmie Brown of Oliver came into my wife's possession because it contained much family material: names and addresses of sons and daughters who had gone abroad, the name, number and military address of his youngest son in the trenches, followed by the date and place where he was killed in action in the 1914–18 war.

'Buisting' was very important and was done immediately the sheep had been clipped. The marking material originally used was always Archangel tar kept thin by heating over a good hot fire. If the fire got low, some tar would be droppd onto the coal to make it blaze up. Jim and I always enjoyed that part. The pot was suspended over the fire on a tripod arrangement using a chain and hook. Sometimes the fire was near a wall and the pot was hung on a swey similar to those used in the cottage fireplaces.

The buister was usually a boy and he might even have been given the day off school to help. Jim and I buisted the 2,000 or more sheep at Hearthstane every year with additional days at other farms. Jim sometimes went to Patervan and I to Badlieu. The actual 'buist' consisted of the initials either of the farm or the farmer. The letters were a standard size, about 3 inches in height, at the end of a 2-foot iron shaft attached to a wooden handle. Hearthstane had been allocated the letters WTFH, but this proved quite impractical and it was reduced to WT, for William Thorburn, the farmer. There had to be at least two of these implements in use at a time, one heating while the other was in use.

The 'buister' had to operate quickly and with great skill, first dipping the 'buist' into the liquid tar and then reaching his objective before the tar had hardened. It was very important to apply the mark correctly to that part of the sheep indicating the farm or hirsel. This could be on the rib, flank or hip of the animal and on either its 'near' (right) or 'far' (left) side. If an animal's skin had been cut in shearing, the tar when applied to the cut and the surrounding area acted as a protection against fly strike and allowed the cut to heal.

Until the middle of the nineteenth century sheep would be smeared with tar and grease to keep out the cold. Although this no longer takes place, evidence of its practice can still be found in some old buildings, long abandoned as smearing houses and now used as stores and keb houses.

In those days the smearing house was a scene of continuous and odorous activity for weeks on end in the autumn. The smearing house had a fireplace of sorts with a swey (protruding arm) or some other arrangement to hold the large three-legged pot for heating the smearing mixture of tallow and Archangel tar. This was spread on the backs of the sheep with a broad piece of wood shaped into a handle at one end. The work was slow as the wool had to be shed at several places along the back and the mixture spread next to the skin. A team of two or three could smear only four or five sheep per hour.

The floor of these stone-built structures was always causewayed. A skilful arrangement of stones on a sand base formed a surface strong enough to stand unending wear and also provide sure footing for the animals. Originally the roof would be thatch but slated roofs replaced these wherever slate was available. One feature in most of them was a 'lunkie', an opening in the wall just big enough to let in one sheep at a time and through which the newly smeared sheep was released.

It is doubtful if the smearing accomplished its purpose. Certainly it spoilt a great deal of wool and made cleaning a lengthy process. However, the wool of the blackface sheep of those times was over a foot long when sheared so that the smeared wool represented only an inch or two on the strands. The wool on the sides and under parts was free from the smearing mixture and was part-cleaned in the washing pool before leaving the sheep.

The washing pools are still identifiable near most of our farms. One characteristic of these pools is a steep side, usually rocky, where the sheep could not escape without swimming some distance after being pushed into the water. Likewise each pool had a gravel bank as an easy landing place.

Sitting on the filled woolsacks waiting for sheep to dry off after a shower, the shepherds could be depended on to recount tales and recall their experiences. Many of these men were native to the Border glens and spoke Border Lallans. One subject that came up for discussion was sheep diseases and their treatment, if not their cures. The explanation of deficiency of minerals and trace elements was only dawning as a cause of illness. Terms like staggers, flake, poke and braxy in sheep, and joint ill, dry neck, watery brash, and grass sickness in lambs were still in use though little understood.

Use of disinfectants came first as the herds saw infections developing into epidemics, often in the same places. On Craiglaw, for example, the name 'Sickness Stell' told its own story, and the parrocks (small enclosures) there were eventually completely deserted. When a sheep went off its feed, the universal practice then was to dose it with what we called 'Kiers', a mixture of treacle, salt, oatmeal and water. It sometimes worked.

Bottled mixtures soon came on the market, and the arrival of the hypodermic syringe, antibiotics, vaccines and a whole range of preventative products revolutionised sheep farming to a point where the art of 'kenning' sheep is no longer needed. Mass housing and food control have meant that traditional skills survive only in a few pockets where sheep still live in natural surroundings.

II

Many centuries ago the first sheep introduced to this area, then part of the great Caledonian Forest, must have had a very varied diet. As well as grass and heather there were twigs and shoots of rowan, birch, hazel, pine, saugh (willow) and juniper, all of which contained elements which are now supplied artificially. After heavy snows when the protruding shoots became scarce, the sheep would naturally start stripping the bark off the older trees. Bark, of course, is quite nourishing and rich in minerals from the soil but its loss would have speeded up the deforestation of the land.

On ground where bent grasses have dominated the herbage for very long periods, heather seems to have disappeared, yet as soon as sheep are excluded, heather reappears and in places the tiny saughs push their red shoots up above the smothering grasses. Having been kept hard-cropped to the ground for so long, they look like dwarf varieties but, given the chance, they at once grow into ordinary specimens.

In Tweedsmuir sheep have eliminated the junipers entirely and only one name, 'Glenheurie', tells where they once abounded. Rowans survived wherever the sheep could not reach them, mainly in rocks and gullies. Birches and hazels have managed to avoid extinction in only a few diminishing sites. A remnant of the old Caledonian Forest remained until quite recent times on Kingledores Hill behind the Crook Inn where an ancient track can be seen. It consisted of old hazels and straggling birches. As boys we gathered the nuts but seldom found ripe kernels. There was a similar relic in the 'Nut Wood' but larches had been added in the early 1880s.

As to medicinal plants, Jim and I took part in an annual event which we never quite understood. In late spring or early summer an elderly farmer arrived at Hearthstane from some place near Biggar. He came in an old dogcart without any prior notice, and his purpose was to gather a few bagfuls of one particular plant. Jim and I knew where the plant grew in White Rig Wood. It was a very coarse grass with broad, flat leaves partly evergreen except for the tops which became rich orange in autumn and winter.

One half of this wood was once blown down and had to be completely cut and cleared. It was replanted with larch and the plant established itself in clumps on the stumps of the original trees. Although we were very young, we were enlisted in the project and helped to gather the coarse greenery. Apparently it was to be used in making a medicinal infusion capable of curing, or perhaps preventing, some illness in the farmer's cows. Every year for many years he arrived at about the same date, so we naturally presumed that the treatment had been successful, though somewhat surrounded in secrecy.

Until the coming of lorries as a means of transport, sheep had to travel on their own four feet. This was still the case when we came to Hearthstane in 1910. Tweedsmuir animals were sold in three main markets: Biggar, Peebles and Lanark. It took a whole day to reach Peebles or Lanark, and this involved staying overnight with the flock ready for the sale the next day.

Biggar was nearer and could be reached in time for the sale if an early start was made. The route led over the ridges running parallel with the Tweed, Holmswater and Kilbucho, following passes and well-marked tracks leaving the Tweed valley at the Logan. This route had been used in earlier times when Skirling Fair, Falkirk Tryst and Dalkeith Fair were the main places for buying and selling livestock.

Peebles was reached by a track from Tweedsmuir through Hearthstane, Polmood and Patervan where it joined a track along the hillfoot to Hopecarton and on to the road which it followed to Dawyck where a droving track continued to Haswellsykes and Barns, with the alternative of crossing by Manor Bridge and continuing over the Swire into Peebles. As a great many droves arrived for the following day's sale, they had to be kept apart in separate enclosures. In the event of insufficient fields, shepherds sometimes had to stay all night with their charges.

Dogs were trained specially for droving, and a dependable one that would 'gang afore' was desirable. This dog would precede the drove, making sure that no members of the flock mixed with any other. Identifying marks enabled any mix-ups to be rectified, and if more

Hay making. Jim Anderson and his father.

than one category was included in the drive, they could be separated before the sale in the shedders (pens) near the ring.

The marks were often strips of colours painted on the horns. Favourite colours were always red, blue, black and even white and had to be easily seen by the operator of the shedder gates. This was fairly easy with blackfaces but the hornless white-faced cheviots were much more difficult to mark. Dots of colour on suitable parts of the face were kept as small as possible to avoid spoiling the appearence, especially of ewe lambs which traditionally were given a mark behind the head where the long body wool began.

Both blackface and cheviot animals had their registered stock marks cut in their ears. Age marks included horn cuts or numbers burnt into the horns. Horned breeds could have burnt stock marks while hornless breeds could be skin-burnt in places with short hair, such as cheeks or ears.

Transport by rail became possible for longer journeys such as to Lanark or Peebles but Tweedsmuir was too far away from the station, and the drove roads continued to be used until road transport overtook other methods. One year an outbreak of foot and mouth disease closed the district, which included Lanark, and movement of livestock was prohibited. The sales were then held at Symington and the droves used the route over into Glenholm and Kilbucho.

Great droves came across the hills from Megget and stayed overnight at Hearthstane. In charge were two well-known personalities, Mick

Little from Meggethead and Willie Laidlaw from Syart. To our youthful eyes they seemed quite elderly but this was probably because they both had beards which obscured most of their features.

Droving required early starting at first light and at times of the year when it could be very cold. We boys often helped to keep the lambs from scattering at the beginning of their journey but we had to return home after a few miles, sometimes unwillingly, when the drove had settled down to a steady pace.

As a youth a day at the sheep sales was a very special and interesting event with the bustle in the pens, the 'sing' of the sellers in their efforts to make their animals show to advantage, the almost unnoticeable ways of conveying bids to the auctioneer, all leading up to the final thump of the gavel with 'sold to so-and-so' followed by the price and hurried departure of the flock with the next lot close behind.

One of my earliest memories of a sheep sale is of fragments of a conversation that I overheard from a group of herds at a pen next to that of Hearthstane. The pen was clearly marked 'Moor Foot' but I soon learned that to the shepherds it was 'Muir Fuit' in Lallans. In the group a very old, slightly bent figure stood several inches taller than any of the others. Moor Foot belonged to the noble Rosebery family and the title 'Earl' drifted several times into the range of our hearing. It was not, however, Lord Rosebery, who owned the land, who was being discussed but a famous blackface tup, a record-breaker at that time. The patriarch of the group never once referred to this famous animal except as the 'Yirl'. He must have inherited the use of the name from his forebears and one couldn't help thinking of the 'yarls' who brought the name across the wild North Sea.

Sheep were kept on the Tweedsmuir hills from quite early times but intensive stocking only began in the seventeenth century. By the next century when the tenure of land had become more stabilised and enclosures had begun to be made, the draining of marshy hill land was a practical method of improving grazing to support higher numbers of sheep.

The planning of drainage systems became very important and re-quired on-the-spot study of slopes and soil types. The outflow and angle of flows had to be judged, as these would affect the speed of the water and the eroding power of the main drains. Many of the early open drains on the hills are still working and have been recut again and again through the centuries. As with the old drove roads and peat roads, they remain as a legacy of our ancestors' work.

The draining work was done largely by employing extra unattached labourers who were paid by the yard rather than the hour. The work was arduous but men could always be found with the skill to undertake the task and who could master all types of terrain. There was usually a source of water at hand, much needed by the sweating workmen, but many of them had a most unusual way of warding off drouth (thirst). They kept a small piece of chuckie (quartz) in their mouths which gradually became smaller, rounder and smoother as saliva slowly dissolved the minerals. It was then replaced by a new white pebble.

The tools consisted of three basic items, a ritter, a hack and a draining spade, with the occasional use of a pick. The ritter was a heavy, triangular, winged spade with the lower slope sharpened to cut through soil or peat. The shaft was short with a wide cross bar for two-handed use. Using the foot on the cutting wing, pressing and guiding with the bar, the operator could keep moving and cutting with a considerable

Davie Murray with his dog and a lamb.

slope inwards. The next move was cutting the other side of the drain so that, while more than a foot wide at ground level, the bottom would be about six inches across. The sloping sides of the drains allowed creatures like lambs and young grouse to climb out safely.

The hack had three or four prongs pointed slightly backwards on a curved shaft to provide leverage when pulling out the material between the two ritter cuts. This often came out as a continuous piece and lay alongside the drain like a long, never-ending snake. The blade of the draining spade was long, pointed and narrow, sloping forward from the shaft to slide along the bottom of the newly cut drain, taking out any left-over debris and levelling the run.

The ultimate object of a system of evenly running drains could usually be obtained by cutting deeper in some places than in others, and here one of the greatest problems could arise. At varying depths there occurs a hard layer between topsoil and subsoil, usually referred to as the 'hard pan'. If this is broken right through, the running

John Fleming, shepherd, at the Manse Glebe.

water cuts down and makes over-deep furrows which expand into deep and dangerous scars or fissures. Similar results occur when too much water is diverted into a main drain, especially if its course is steeply downhill.

Drains too straight downhill on steep slopes simply meant that in a few years the water would cut a deep channel with subsequent erosion. In such instances, if the terrain permitted, a long 'swaip' (slanting) drain was made at an angle which allowed a sufficient run to keep the water flowing but not so fast that it would cut deeply into the ground. Where long drains were impracticable, ziz-zag patterns at just the right angle were equally successful.

Sheep drains kept functioning well on some hills for fifty years or more but eventually they became blocked with vegetation growing inwards over the bulging sides. The drains then had to be 'cleaned'. This involved cutting the sides with the ritter and cleansing the bottom with the draining spade. Two sods, one on each side, had to be hauled

Thomas Lorimer and
William Anderson.

out with the hack, and this could sometimes be slower and harder than making the original drain.

The coming of the machine age made it possible to cut new drains, or indeed to clear old ones, at speed, and eventually the mechanical draining machine took over from the human craftsman. These machines could go anywhere passable by a crawling tractor and could cut to any depth through soft peat or hard subsoil with equal ease. In fact a better result was obtained by cutting new drains, and these sometimes appeared alongside the old ones, sometimes crossing them, but always deeper. Over-deep cutting destroyed the 'hard pan' and created many permanent hazards with deep traps for lambs in snow.

Examples of well-drained hills with their distinctive patterns are to be found on most Border hills. Crossing from Megget to Talla, one looks straight into the face of Carlavin Hill where a drainage system has survived at least a century with a ziz-zag pattern on a steep wet slope and is still as effective as when first cut. On another farm in the district a 'swaip' drain has been extended quite unnecessarily to collect so much water into a downhill watercourse that an impassable gorge now extends to several hundred yards. On another mechanical drainage has so increased the flow in the runnel draining a wide basin-shaped hollow that the eroded watercourse trapped a heft of sheep which needed to cross it in a snowstorm and more than half were lost.

Several other examples of badly planned drainage can be seen on sheep farms, and sometimes heaps of gravel and soil indicate the amount of resulting erosion. The impact of the mechanical age on our hills came to a climax with forestry ploughing, forestry roads and planting. Much of the evidence of the work of our forebears to improve the land for their sheep has now been obliterated.

Where a long glen formed an integral part of a large farm, the furthest part was referred to as 'oot bye' ground. This land was tended by a shepherd living in a cottage strategically situated beside a burn within the bounds of the herding. These 'oot bye' shepherds have entirely disappeared from the farming scene and their cottages, far up the glens, are now 'rickles o' stanes' (heaps of stones) or seasonal holiday homes. Such remote herdings were latterly less favoured by families with schoolchildren, yet some shepherds preferred these lonely outposts as they were allowed to keep extra animals as long as they provided their winter feeding.

Their cottages consisted of the usual 'but and ben' with a byre built on to one end. At the rear an abutment formed a scullery and milk house with a dry toilet and stone-built pigsty spaced out along the back walls. The peat stack might lean against the byre but the haystack, hen house and midden (dung heap) occupied suitable adjacent situations.

The work of these shepherds varied with the seasons but one general rule of herding as then practised consisted of bringing the sheep down from the hills in the morning and driving them back up again before nightfall, making sure that they kept to their own hefts even in lambing time and especially at tup time. This routine was only broken by the rigours of winter. Snowstorms fully tested the herd's abilities as he had to rely on his weather forecasting and judgment in order to have his charges in the safest places where they might survive the impending blizzards.

The most critical time of the year came in late spring when lambing began and occupied the shepherd all the daylight hours. Although extra help might be given by a 'lambing man' during the three-week peak period, it was still a very demanding time. As the sheep remained spread out over the whole hill and gave birth over a widely scattered area, every part had to be visited two or three times a day.

Within a few weeks of lambing, depending on the weather, work began on cutting the peat. This involved both the shepherd and his wife until the peat was finally stacked beside the house. Haymaking followed when sufficient had to be made to feed the animals through the winter. This also involved both the shepherd and his wife. In addition the herd had to attend numerous local handlings, markings, dippings, clippings, speaning and finally the markets.

Shearing took up a lot of time, for 'neighbouring' was then general. This meant the shepherd had to go to all the surrounding farms in return for their communal help with his own flock. In bad weather this could be a very frustrating and trying time, not only for the shepherd but also for his wife who then had to attend to all the work on her own, even sometimes going to the hill.

Life in these outlying sheilings was lonely for the shepherds' wives and families. The men quite often met neighbouring shepherds on their boundaries but their wives hardly ever saw anyone except their spouses. Many marches (boundaries) were open and sheep could be driven by wind and storm on to neighbouring ground or strayed in search of better grazing. The shepherds, in searching for missing animals or returning strays, had opportunities for meeting. To prevent trespass one hirsel would be herded against the other. In this way the grazing would be equally used on both sides of the boundary and the sheep would not be tempted to think the grass was better on one side than the other. This too brought shepherds into closer contact, but not their wives and families.

If a village could be reached by walking, social events might be attended, but independently of organised occasions another form of entertainment was practised among outlying herds. This was the 'basket nicht' (basket night) when neighbouring households made reciprocal trips over the intervening hills to each others' homes, taking with them a basket containing enough food, and sometimes drink, to avert any undue strain on the host household.

The period between tup time and lambing time was especially favoured for these basket nights, although late autumn after the sheep sales but before tup time also provided a short spell when the shepherds' work was less pressing. This avoided the longest nights of winter and the worst weather although sometimes the New Year was chosen. These visits always took place when the moon was full enough to light the travellers on their way home in the early hours.

Such nights were important events in the lives of these lonely families. Most homes had a fiddle and the basket nights passed quickly with music, singing and dancing. Even games of cards were played including the favourites 'Catch the Ten' and 'Rummy'. Halfway through the evening came the supper, partly provided from the 'basket' and accompanied by a dram or two. Something had to be left in the bottle for 'Deoch an' Doris' before the long walk home across the hill. These nights, rare and memorable, became recurrent subjects of conversation among the participants throughout their lifetimes.

A good stock of hay was essential for feeding the animals throughout the long and often very severe winters. Farms in the lower part of the valley had fields reserved for hay. The upper part of the parish was mainly mossy moorland with only small enclosed meadows for hay. These often consisted of mixed wild grasses and sprett, a hollow rush which needed dampish conditions. Even blow bent (a coarse type of grass) was sometimes mown. These grasses could only be mown (scythed) when damp, and this meant rising early and starting at dawn. When the sun rose and the standing grass dried, even the sharpest scythe became useless.

This damp grass was the home of hordes of angry midges which attacked the disturbers of their peace with determined ferocity. There was however a complete cure at hand – sweat – and plenty of it. Any youthful complaint elicited the advice of experience, 'ca harder laddie, ca harder an' dinna stop'.

Before the construction of the Talla and Fruid reservoirs both areas had shallow lakes filled up with deposits from the surrounding hills, known as Talla Lake and Fruid Lake. These were in fact deep bogs but were often covered by floodwater, especially in winter. In summer these bogs dried out sufficiently for the grassier parts to be mown for hay. This bog hay was a mixture of marsh grasses, rushes (sprett) and other less edible plants, especially meadowsweet which flourished in the wetter parts. Today's farmers would be surprised that livestock depended on this product for their survival in winter.

The hay had to be scythed laboriously in the accessible parts and then, because of the dampness of the ground, taken out to the lowest parts of the surrounding hills to dry off. Great bundles of moist hay were carried in sheets of sacking material by the men, stripped to the waist, who vied with each other as to who could handle the biggest load.

At Talla much of the crop was dried on the south-facing ground at the foot of Talla Banks but some very rough, weedy hay was made annually on the Garelet side. This was built into a stack on a piece of flat ground above the flood level between the Menzion boundary and the confluence of Old Talla with Gameshope Burn. In some winters much of the stack was used, but when none was used the farmer made the hay as usual and built it on top of the old. This went on year after year until the stack became a standing joke among the young shepherds. Although added to regularly, the haystack never seemed to grow owing to the drying out and compression of the old material at the bottom into hard brown layers.

This stack, which had come to be regarded as something of a 'folly', finally justified its existence in the great snowstorm of 1890 when large numbers of sheep starved to death and others had to be moved from the hills to lower land where fodder was available. The Garelet sheep were fed round the now notorious stack which soon began to disappear, and by the time the thaw came it had shrunk, brown layers and all, to ground level. The Garelet sheep came through the storm without casualties and, as the late John Robertson (who was born at Over Menzion and farmed in Tweedsmuir for many years) recalled, all that was left of the stack were the inedible stumps of the meadowsweet which had 'bedded the ground a' roond aboot wi' bits a' stuff like thousands o' scartit spunks (sparks of fire)'.

Farms further down the valley had arable land as well as hill land, and when my family came to Tweedsmuir these farms were often tenanted and held on leases of various lengths from about 7 years upwards. One condition that was always written into the lease was that crops would be grown in a certain rotation covering a fixed number of years for each crop and that the land must be under a root crop at least once in each rotation. This crop was usually turnips, after which the field would be the 'cleaned land' suitable for grain and eventually grass.

This was the 'horse age' of farming, going back to before the First World War and before the time of tractors. Looking back, the amount of work involved would shock present-day farmers. First of all came ploughing, as the field would probably be in stubble after grain, which in Peeblesshire was usually oats. This would be single furrow with a pair of Clydesdales and done in winter or the end of autumn to let the frost break up the soil.

Sowing time for turnips was later than for grain, and the first process was grubbing and took at least two operations, one following the furrows and another across. If any areas were affected with couch grass, they would be harrowed until all had come to the surface. Next came harrowing with ordinary harrows which broke the soil into a tilth suitable for sowing. If however there was too much couch grass, chain harrows were used which left the drying couch roots in rolls which were then lifted with forks into heaps and burnt.

The land was now ready for ridging with the swing plough. This plough had two equal wings and formed equal ridges but took much skill and strength. One good steady horse was needed. The turnip seed was then sown in a groove made on the top of the ridge by a machine which made the groove, dropped in the seed and rolled the top of the ridge. As soon as the seedlings were strong enough, 'singling' began and this was a very important operation. Using 'draw hoes', a team cut out the surplus plants, leaving one about every 9 inches, and at the same time any weeds were pulled down into the fur (furrow) between the ridges. This was the main cleaning action, for the space between the lines was 'hurkled' (horse-hoed) as soon after singling as possible in order to kill the weeds. Hurkles were frames with small tines which covered only the ground between the rows. Hurkling could be repeated if necessary until the plants had spread out their leaves.

'Shawing' began in early winter when the plants had reached their full size and the leaves had shrunk a bit. This was tiring work, as each turnip had to be pulled up, the tail cut, then severed from the shaws and landed in line with other lines for easy lifting. This was all done in one turning movement as one moved along the row. Then came carting with box carts, heaving the turnips up to the level of the load and tipping them into clamps near the steading. From here they could be barrowed to the cutter which reduced them to slices. These were then usually carried in spale (wood) baskets to the troughs.

For this crop there were eight horse operations and six hand tasks compared with only seven mechanical operations nowadays. Weeks of hard hand work entailing heavy physical effort have now been replaced by only hours of machinery work. Singling required skill, shawing took both skill and accuracy as well as strength, loading carts was back-breaking, especially if the turnips were large and heavy. In wet weather deep ruts and mud made carting difficult, and wet muddy roots handled with cold, numbed fingers added to the misery of the workers. My father used to tell of shawing on a field at Hamildean which was so steep that all the turnips rolled to the bottom ready for collection and carting to the farmyard.

Farming has completely changed over the years, and modern methods and machinery have revolutionised the work in the valley. The old farming communities are no more, many of the higher parts are now forestry plantations, and many of those living in the valley no longer get their living from the land. I was fortunate to have known the valley from before the 1914–18 war and to have been told of the life and ways before my time.

Chapter Six *Cottage Life*

The two shepherds' cottages at Hearthstane, occupied by Jim Anderson's family and my own, were well built and semi-detached with two storeys instead of the usual 'but and ben' style. They had been built at right angles to the burn with walled gardens behind and were flanked by the cow byres some distance away.

When my family moved there in 1910, shepherds' cash wages were between 16/– and 18/– per week. These families more or less lived on the produce of their cows, their hens and their pigs and the meal and potatoes allowed as part of their 'bargain', the conditions of their employment.

Most married shepherds were allowed to have a 'pack', a few sheep of their own, as part of their bargain. Those on outlying farms could keep extra animals but they had to provide all their winter fodder. These packs were a valuable addition to a shepherd's income, providing lambs, wool and occasionally meat.

'Fallen wool' from the farmer's flock was also part of the shepherd's bargain. Even without a pack a fair amount of wool was obtained when sheep, already beginning to lose their coats, passed along paths in long heather or 'birns' (strong stems which had survived burning), leaving parts of their fleeces stuck on the twigs. When sheep died on the hill, especially at lambing time, they were not buried immediately and their wool, like that of dead lambs, could be stripped (sloughed) from their bodies. All this wool was sent off to the mills and made into cloth, blankets or knitting yarn.

Farm workers kept pigs to provide themselves with meat all the year round. Sometimes two pigs were kept, one to be killed and the second to be sold to pay for the feeding of both. Much of the pig food consisted of potatoes and skim milk which the pigs enjoyed even though it was 'lappered' (coagulated).

Pigs could only be killed in the cold months, those with an R in the name, but not September which was often too warm. Pig killing was quite a complicated job and needed much preparation. Knives had to be sharpened, straw laid out and the fire made strong enough to boil up the pots and kettles of water needed for scalding the hair before shaving it off. If black puddings were to be made, a large bowl had to be at hand to catch the blood. A strong rope and a 'hangarell' were also required. A hangarell was a strong, curved bar of wood to which the rope was attached, and this would hold the carcass up by the hind legs from the rafters or the upper rungs of a ladder.

The actual slaughter of the animal was not a spectacle for the squeamish. Getting the pig from its sty to the laid-out straw was often quite difficult and noisy. Rendered unconscious by a blow from the back of a heavy axe, the pig was immediately bled by an incision in the throat so deep that the knife, which was especially long and sharp, reached the heart. This allowed nearly all the animal's blood to be drained away or collected in a vessel if wanted.

Next came the scraping with kettles of scalding water poured on the skin to allow the hair to be cut right at the skin, leaving it clean and white except for the wrinkles round the face. The hangarell was then fitted behind the sinews of the back legs and the whole carcass raised clear of the ground either by looping the rope over the rafters or over the upper rungs of an almost perpendicular ladder or even a branch of a tree.

Cutting and disembowelling was a skilful operation and was usually carried out by someone with much experience. At Hearthstane this was undertaken by Jim's father, Archie Anderson. Unwanted parts of the intestines were taken away and buried but some were steeped in salt water and cleaned in the running water of the burn. Now perfectly clean, these could be used for making white puddings with an oatmeal filling which was highly spiced and rich or for black puddings made mainly with blood. These puddings were cooked and partly dried for future use. The liver was used almost immediately.

Everyone made 'potted head'. The head of the pig was too difficult to skin properly so it was singed, pronounced 'sing'it'. If one lived near a smithy, this was done by the blacksmith, but a good red hot poker did the job at Hearthstane. Sometimes half a cow's head from the butcher was added to the pot. After much boiling the bits of meat were all cut from the bones. These pieces of meat and fat were put through the mincer with pepper and salt when still hot and then put into bowls. When cold, the contents could be turned out for immediate use or left in their containers until required. Sometimes even the trotters were cooked and the bones made a very palatable white jelly. Pig cheeks, which looked very fat and oily, were very good when fried or grilled.

When stiff and cold, the carcass was cut up and put in tubs for a few days and kept covered in salt brine. Later these joints were put on the milkhouse shelves where they were rubbed with salt and turned daily. When cured, each was put in a cheesecloth bag ready to hang from the 'kipples' (rafters). These joints would now provide ham and bacon throughout the year.

Shepherds were also allowed as part of their bargain to kill at least one 'eild' (old) ewe per year. The ewe was always one that had failed to produce a lamb for at least two seasons and was therefore in extremely good condition. At clipping time a sheep was killed to provide food for the shearers. The actual killing was similar to that of the pigs but simpler, and the head was always made into broth. Singeing was also necessary and this gave the 'kail' (dish) a most distinctive flavour.

As well as pork and lamb we had rabbits and hares for meat, and the river and burns provided trout and salmon. The taking of salmon was supposed to be illegal during the closed season, which was the only time they were present in the upper reaches. Tradition survived from times when fresh runs supplied much of each winter's food stores, and it was almost an unwritten obligation for the menfolk to provide fish for use and to store either salted or 'reested' (dried). I will describe our fishing techniques elsewhere but for the present it will suffice to say that our larders were not devoid of fish.

When coal became scarce and expensive during the 1914–18 war, we had to burn peat and wood. I have described in an earlier chapter how we opened up the old peat faces and gathered wood at Hearthstane. Further up the valley peat had always been used, as it could be dug on lower and more accessible parts of the hills. We children found it fun to help with collecting this fuel after school, on Saturdays and in the holidays and get it safely stacked by our homes.

Ground to grow potatoes was provided by the farmer but the shepherds had to supply their own seed. Planting day was a day of communal activity with everyone helping, sometimes even the women. Equal numbers of lines were assigned to the shepherds and the ploughman, and rather more to the farmhouse, supposedly because the young unmarried shepherd stayed there.

During the summer the rows of potatoes usually had to be hoed to kill the weeds but my father always insisted that this should be done whether there were weeds or not. I thought this very unnecessary but it seemed to give better results when the potatoes were ploughed out in the autumn.

The crop was stored in a pit dug about 6 inches deep and about 4 feet wide. The potatoes were built up to a steep top which was covered with straw or bracken and some soil. The outside was clad with peaty sods placed with the growth outwards to make a frost-proof store. If we had any spare late cabbages, a few were tucked into the end and covered well with insulating material. These came out in spring or late winter and after the outer leaves were removed proved perfectly good.

My father told of an unusual incident which happened when he was a small boy at Blyth Bridge and was sent to keep crows away from a crop of potatoes. As he had to be at the field before the crows, he had to start quite early. One day as he went round the outside of the lines of potatoes, he noticed what looked like a spikey branch sticking up between two rows of the crop. It proved to be a full-horned stag which had hoped to spend the day in peace. My father hurried home to get someone to kill it but no one believed him, so the animal got away unscathed.

As boys our diet contained a large amount of oatmeal, eaten mainly in the form of porridge. Shepherds, as part of their bargain, received several bags of oatmeal and flour delivered at special dates. We school-children often had porridge twice a day. There was always porridge for supper, and I loved having it again in the morning heated up with milk, preferring it to the usual egg or the occasional slice of ham which other members of the family had for their breakfast.

All the housewives baked scones on girdles suspended from the 'swey', an iron bar above the stove. These scones were shaped from rounds which had been cut crosswise to form four triangular pieces baked on both sides. Some households had ovens, and scones baked in these ovens did not have to be turned over. Sometimes the scones were fried with or after cooking ham and eggs. Pancakes or dropped scones containing eggs were also made on the girdle. These were a delicacy, and occasionally currants were added to the mixture as a special treat. Oatcakes were also cooked on the girdle and finished on a grill in front of the fire where they dried and curled. Scones and pancakes were eaten at teatime which was about half-past four or five o'clock when we got back from school. Sometimes there was a bottle of coffee extract called 'Camp', but it was only used if other beverages were not available.

Both my family and Jim's, the Andersons, kept a cow. The cow field occupied both sides of the Hearthstane Burn and was bounded by the River Tweed. As the cows had to pass in front of the cottages

Hearthstane Cottages.

to and from their pasture, there was a certain amount of co-operation between the two families so both cows could be moved together at milking time.

As a rule cows had a dry spell after lactation and before calving, but at lambing time they had to be in full milk to provide emergency feeding for the lambs. The two households always managed to arrange that the two cows were never dry at the same time.

Butter making involved much preparation. For several days cream was skimmed from the milk and gathered in a large glazed earthenware crock. In cold weather it had to be put near the fire to induce the slight bacterial action necessary for churning. The gathered cream was then transferred to the wooden churn and the real work began.

If conditions were just right, butter would form in less than half an hour, if not the splashing paddles would have to be turned for hours and sometimes only granules of butter would be produced. As an emergency measure these could be put through fine gauze to squeeze the particles together but the process was unsatisfactory as it was difficult to get rid of the buttermilk.

When the butter came out of the churn the butter spades came into use, pressing out excess liquid and forming rectangular or round blocks weighing about half a pound. The final finish came with the spades or a butter stamp producing a pattern on the top. Work was not over, however, as the remaining buttermilk had to be emptied from the churn and stored in an earthenware pot for baking or drinking and the churn itself dismantled and thoroughly scoured and dried ready for the next batch of cream.

At one time we shared a cheese press with the Andersons. To make cheese on a small scale a certain amount of milk had to be obtained all in one batch. This was only possible by using the milk from both the Anderson's cow and ours. This milk had to be soured and the resultant thick curd squeezed in the press until all the whey was extracted. The cheese was then covered and dried but it never turned out as it should, which was a great disappointment.

There was more success with preserving surplus eggs from our hens. These were put in big jars containing isinglass and could be used when the hens stopped laying or when it was more profitable to sell the new-laid ones.

There was always a garden attached to the shepherds' houses which provided early potatoes, cabbages, curly greens and sometimes beet and peas. Cauliflowers were unknown in these cottage gardens. There was also bush fruit like black and red currants and sometimes gooseberries, but these did not always fruit. Strawberries and raspberries were practically unknown, as were apple and plum trees.

Rhubarb grew well and was a mainstay for jam which was usually made plain but sometimes with ginger or even figs. Some years we got small blue damsons from Clydeside and Victoria plums for jam making. During the 1914–18 war sugar became very scarce and some people tried to bottle fruit to preserve it without using sugar. Groups of households sometimes joined in schemes for obtaining jars and bottling their soft fruit. When jam was scarce, we had syrup or treacle for a change.

Some wild plants provided us with other delicacies. 'Arnuts' were a favourite. These were rough-shaped tubers found at the foot of the stem of the plant, about an inch or two underground. They could be dug up quite easily with a strong knife. Sometimes they were no bigger than a marble and didn't look very appetising covered in soil. A good 'dicht' (rub) on a jacket sleeve dislodged most of the dirt and also the brown outer skin and, hey presto, there was a lovely fresh, chewy nut with a really strong nutty flavour. Some wild animals, especially the wild swine, knew the secret of arnuts, and in hard times pheasants dig them up.

When the new, pale green seeds grew on the elm trees before the leaves appeared, we pulled these off in small bunches and ate them like a salad. If picked at the best stage, they were bland and juicy but they were in season for only a short time before the wing part became dry and brown.

Hazel nuts seldom had full kernels, and very few trees remained where once they had abounded. A few grew on Kingledores behind the Crook, a few at Polmood and there was a Nut Wood at Mossfennan a bit further away.

Sow thistles grew at one place beside the Tweed at the Wisdom Pool. The purple florets grew out of a pad of what we called 'thistle cheese', probably because of its texture when eaten. When the covering skin was removed, there was very little left to eat, but eat it we did and without ill effects. In a few places wild roses produced scarlet dog hips. These too were edible when ripe but once the seeds were discarded there was little left to eat.

On the hills we found blaeberries and crowberries most years but the best were the cloudberries which grew only on the high peaty tops. These were the berries which one year we picked to give to the school inspector. They were always ripe at the end of July and the beginning of August and were yellowish-purple in colour. We never seemed able to collect enough to make jam but one year I got about one pound or so which I carried home in my hat. How I came to have a hat I cannot remember as I never wore one unless it was raining. There weren't enough to make into jam and my mother made turnovers with them. The stones would not have suited false teeth and the taste reminded one of very strong almonds.

We found two varieties of cranberries. One was bright red with dark, glossy foliage and cropped only in very good years. The second, with thin, red, thread-like runners and tiny leaves, grew on wet, peaty ground and was so difficult to find that few people knew of its existence. It could be found near the curling pond and the berries were more easily seen when unripe and red. When ripe, there were never enough of the purplish berries to be worth collecting.

One of my brothers was a shepherd at Badlieu, some six miles further up the valley. As I grew older I was encouraged to go there to help with the sheep at dipping and clippings. I was also attracted to Badlieu because of my early addiction to fishing. The shepherd's house at Badlieu was typical of the 'but and ben' cottage of the time, a type that has long since disappeared. 'But and ben' meant two main rooms with a ladder to a very low attic lit only by two small skylights. Slate, from the large slate quarries at Stobo, had replaced the former thatch roof. A byre was built on to one gable end and there was space beyond for a haystack. An arched tin shed was built later. At the back of the house was a lean-to kennel, a wooden hen house, a small pigsty built of stone and the necessary dry privy. Further away from the back door the dung heap and the ash pit were side by side. The peat ash often kept smouldering even though the residue looked merely a dry, red powder.

Inside the cottage the peat fire burned in a hearth with a swey. This consisted of an upright iron shaft which ran from floor to mantle on one side of the hearth. A swinging bar was attached at right angles at the top of the shaft. From this hung a chain at the end of which was an S-shaped hook which could be swung across the fire. Pots, pans and girdles all had loops on the top so they could be hung from the S-shaped hook over the glowing peats below. Cast iron fireplaces had come into use but at that time this improvement had not been installed in all peat-burning homes.

The floors were stone with a home-made rug in front of the fire. Not far from the fireplace a box-bed had been built against a wall. This was simply a wooden bed with the sides boarded up almost to the ceiling and a door for access in the front. Some box-beds had curtains instead of a door. When visiting as a boy, I slept in the low attic which I shared with a young shepherd.

A feature which was found in many of these isolated sheilings was a small square window in the gable end. This commanded a view of the shepherd's homeward route from the hill. It is still clearly visible at Badlieu from the main road. At the front of the cottage a steep bank falls some 40 yards or so to the burn. On it grew the inevitable rowan tree which was always planted near dwellings as these trees had mystic superstitions attached to them and were supposed to ward off any evil.

A series of well-worn steps slanted from the burn towards the wooden porch which sheltered the draughty front door. Pails of water had to be carried up these steps every day for all cooking and household purposes. Two or three pails of water always stood inside the porch as the burn water was often peaty and only cleared and became usable after standing for a few hours. Our morning ablutions were carried out at the burnside where a piece of red carbolic soap and a tin basin stayed permanently on a large flat rock. It was several years after the 1914–18 war before running water was installed.

Breakfast consisted of bacon fresh cut from a ham taken down from

Glenriskie.

the 'kipples', egg (usually a duck egg) and girdle scones. Tea made with the soft burn water had quite a distinctive flavour, as had the butter. Jam was usually some variation of rhubarb, which grew well even at that altitude. Berry bushes were hardly worth growing as they only bore fruit in very good years.

Shepherds living in isolated cottages such as my brother's at Badlieu often faced difficulties especially in bad weather. In the early years of the war my brother became seriously ill with pneumonia. The doctor from Biggar set out to visit him in his car (one of the very few at that time), but when he got stuck near the Crook Inn my Father arranged to take him to Badlieu in a high-wheeled dog cart. The horse, borrowed from the farm, was a new acquisition, probably an army reject, and looked too big for the vehicle. Nevertheless it rose to the occasion and the doctor and my Father, suitably muffled up, ploughed their way through the deep drifts.

About a mile from Badlieu a huge drift blocked further progress on the road. Some of the high ground which was exposed to the wind had less snow and, abandoning the dog cart, it was possible to continue on foot. The doctor, who was a very short, stout man, was unable to

3.1 Badlieu

3.2 Feeding the Sheep, Horseshoe Wood, Mossfennan

3.3 Shepherd's Warning

3.4 Unexpected Arrivals

3.5 The Challenge

3.6 Mother and Twins

3.7 The Tweed at
Dawyck

3.8 Roe Deer in the
Woods

mount the horse but, with his important bag attached to the saddle, continued the journey on foot with my Father.

The treatment proved successful and, although the illness took a long time to pass, my brother's recovery was complete and he continued to herd until his retirement some 40 years later. The doctor's adventures were all in the day's work for the practitioners of those times and created a strong bond between patient and doctor. Dr Mason's professional visits to our household were treated as events of importance and I always provided a basket of burn trout for him to take home from the grateful family.

Within a few years of coming to Hearthstane my brothers and sisters, apart from Janet, had all grown up and left home. Janet was lame and and worked from home as a rural dressmaker. The household now consisted of Granny, my parents, Janet and myself. My other sisters were nearly all within cycling distance and came home on their half-days off on Sundays.

There was always a full table at the afternoon meal on these occasions and we always had something substantial like rabbit pie or stew. Afterwards the Moody and Sankey Hymn Book was brought out as well as the ordinary Church Hymn Book. Some of my sisters seemed to know several hymns off by heart and we all sang as heartily as we could without any accompaniment. When we later had a gramophone we all joined in singing with our records of hymns and sacred songs like 'Abide with me', the 23rd Psalm and 'The lost Chord'. On these occasions my Father sang something different in Scots to the tune of 'The Auld Hoose'. I can only remember a few lines:

> The rich, the puir, the young, the auld
> Tae Jesus a' the same,
> Come unto me He says tae a'
> An' ye're a' welcome hame.

My Father had a wide repertoire of songs, many of which were the bothy ballad type. There were also the songs of the kirns, those spontaneous harvest celebrations when farmers and workers joined in the event of the year to mark the successful culmination of the season's work. Alas he only sang on rare occasions and I remember some songs like 'Banks of Claddie' only by name, and others like 'Bundle and Go' for their 'going' tune and chorus.

My Mother was very strong, with tremendous energy. She milked the cow, fed the pig, looked after the hens, washed, ironed and mended, helped with collecting wood for the fire, always had meals ready on time and did a thousand other tasks that were taken for granted. She had a great influence on her children who tried to follow the principles which she exemplified: work, honesty, sobriety, thrift, independence and charity to others.

In 1918 when we moved to Glenriskie, which was also part of Hearthstane, about a mile further up the valley, life for my Mother was a little easier but she was still kept very busy. In 1926 my Father retired and he and my Mother moved to Soonhope in Peebles which was to remain their home for the rest of their lives. My brother at Badlieu now took over my Father's work at Hearthstane.

Today our former homes have been greatly altered. The Andersons' cottage and ours adjoining it at Hearthstane have now been made into one dwelling. Glenriskie is no longer part of Hearthstane and has been modernised. Badlieu is now surrounded by forest plantations and the cottage, no longer a shepherd's home, is very different to the old but and ben that I knew so many years ago.

Chapter Seven   *Cadgers, Moudie Men and Others*

Many of my recollections of the years before the First World War and onwards are of people whose work was closely associated with the land or with our country scene. Alas, changes over the years have eliminated many of these occupations and greatly reduced the number employed in others.

I remember vividly the bands of tinkers who would sometimes pass through the valley in their tall, squarish, brightly painted four-wheeled caravans or in the smaller, rounded type. Usually an extra pony and a lurcher or two accompanied the party. They were never very welcome and we children were warned to keep away from them. Nevertheless we had a sneaking admiration for their way of life.

The arrival of the cadgers' carts was quite different and news of their approach always caused a ripple of excitement especially among the children. In the early years of this century the cadger's cart was a common sight on our country roads. The name 'cadger' was not then a derogatory term but simply indicated a merchant who carried his wares to his customers and bought their produce in part exchange. In this way fresh country goods such as eggs and butter could be taken to the surrounding towns.

Specially built horse-drawn carts carried basic necessities to distant households as well as those along the main roads. The most outlying houses could not be reached directly and depended upon a weekly or fortnightly rendezvous at some suitable place or dwelling on the cadger's route. Farms and cottages in the valley up to Tweedsmuir were served by traders from Biggar on a regular basis. Talla, Fruid and Tweed above Tweedsmuir depended upon Moffat traders for supplies. Sometimes representatives were sent round to take orders which were delivered monthly or even quarterly.

One unique trader, Danny Poletti, came from Biggar and, unlike the others, arrived only once or twice a year. To us children his travelling shop was an Aladdin's cave and even its outer appearance conjured up visions of glittering treasures. The rather long, four-wheeled cart, drawn by a demure little pony, may have been a converted gypsy caravan. It was painted all over, gypsy style, in the brightest of colours with lines and patterns extending to the four smallish wheels.

Inside the van tiers of tightly packed shelves stretched from front to back. On the lines of hooks at their edges hung tinkling examples of his wares – pots and pans, brushes of all sorts and sizes, china cups and jugs, as well as miscellaneous articles which had holes or hooks for hanging in their future places of employment. At the back opening of the van were several tin containers filled with paraffin for the lamps which had only recently replaced candles.

Crockery formed a large part of Danny's stock. There were articles ranging in size from great earthenware crocks used for buttermilk, storing salt fish and preserving eggs, to tiny china egg cups. Brightly coloured Japanese punch bowls and 'Wally Dogs' were his speciality. Some may still exist as heirlooms and mementos of those days of barter trading. If a housewife asked for something that was not immediately to hand, Danny would dive into the dark, hidden recesses behind the shelves and, sure enough, the article would eventually be produced in pristine condition.

Danny's ironmongery included cutlery, and in addition he carried a selection of horn spoons. These had been in general use since the beginning of time and were still in favour with older folk and sometimes with younger people too. No two spoons were alike. Some were streaked with black, grey or white in wispy waves through the bowl to the handle and others were pale shades of yellow and brown, with all the intervening hues, depending on the source of the horn from which they were made. These spoons, unlike their metal counterparts, were individuals and porridge tasted better when supped with one's own special spoon.

Danny always came just after lambing time and accepted lamb skins in payment for some articles such as punch bowls. The news of his imminent arrival sent us children off to the keb house and all the parrocks in search of lamb skins. These skins, from lambs which were either still born or had died soon after birth, had served as coats to induce ewes to accept the lambs substituted for their own dead off-spring. As Danny visited nearly every shepherd's house in the glen, he must have had dozens and dozens of lamb skins without any money changing hands. When cured and processed, these skins made a product almost identical to genuine astrakhan, far removed from the punch bowls for which they had been bartered.

One enterprising Moffat cadger, James Reive, left that town about the middle of every week and followed the Selkirk road to St Mary's Loch. At Cappercleugh he turned up the Megget valley where he stayed the night. Continuing up the valley the next day, he carried on over the rough track to Talla and from there his route took him by the Tweed road back to Moffat having after calling at every household on the way.

During and immediately after World War I horses were gradually replaced by motors. Great changes followed, with many more specialised suppliers like grocers, butchers, bakers and even fishmongers competing for custom. The Moffat trader, James Reive, now acquired a Model T Ford and could complete his long route in one day. The most difficult part of his journey was the long, steep descent into Talla. Each week he filled a large box with stones at the top and, using it as a drag, he negotiated the rough gravelly slope and emptied the stones on to an ever-growing heap at the bottom. These stones remained long after the demise of the Model T as a memorial to the determination and ingenuity of James Reive.

A story dating from the middle of the nineteenth century shows how dependent the outlying farms and cottages had always been on the cadgers' visits. Passed down through the generations by word of mouth, it gives an account of the time when the shepherds of Fruid had withstood a particularly long, hard winter. Their stores had run very low as the cadgers had been unable to reach them through the snow.

As soon as the weather began to improve, one of the young shepherds, called McMorran, set out with a horse and cart to replenish their supplies. He took the route of an old cart track which was now just passable. The track, once a reivers' road, started at the head of Fruid Water, led to Carterhope then round the shoulder of Balamans Hill, skirting the head of Glencraigs Burn, crossed Earlshaugh into the head of Annan Water and eventually joined the farm road to Moffat. At one point on Earlshaugh the track passed near a sheep still (shelter) and McMorran noticed something unusual in the lee of the wall. On investigation he found it was the corpse of a 'gaun body' (tramp) who had perished while sheltering from the snow. He lifted the lifeless body into the empty cart and continued on his way to Moffat.

Once in Moffat, McMorran found himself in a quandary as no one was willing to take responsibility for the body. He had found it in the county of Peebles and had brought it to Dumfriesshire. For a while it seemed as though he might have to return it to its original resting place. Eventually he was able to leave and return home with the much-needed stores. From that day no one ever used the track and, in about 1932, when I set out to follow it, I found it had almost disappeared.

Packmen also provided a service to the outlying dwellings and settlements. Some of these wandering salesmen were mere beggars who used their packs as an excuse to put over their professional patter, and often they passed on and were never seen again. Some, however, were genuine traders. The 'pack' consisted of a large coloured sheet filled with their wares and carried over their shoulders. When laid down and opened, it displayed all the goods on offer. The amount of goods, mainly clothing and household articles, was limited to what could be carried in one large bundle. Most packmen had a reserve stock at home, and with the coming of the bicycle more could be carried and a much larger market could be reached.

In Tweedsmuir two of these individuals were regular visitors. One came from Biggar by bicycle and sold mainly soft goods like underclothing. As he couldn't carry a great selection of wares, he made up for this shortage by offering to return the next day with almost any article required. When motor cycles appeared, he bought one with a side car which, of course, gave him more trade. He eventually acquired a shop and built up a high-class drapery business.

The other regular visitor was very different. In fact she was a packwoman. She and her husband came from Dumfriesshire and seemed to be of gypsy extraction. Their name was Kennedy and some called her Kennedy the Tink. She was a most imposing figure, well built and amply proportioned. Her husband was equally robust with a reputation as a 'horse cowper', someone who trained all types of horses, especially wild ones. Their son Frankie, a boy of my age, was usually with them as they arrived at the beginning of the school holidays.

They travelled in a traditional caravan with an extra dog-cart for the 'pack'. They always camped beside a burn, usually Gala Burn or Menzion, or on the banks of the Tweed at Stanhope. With her well-stocked pack Mrs Kennedy visited even the most outlying shielings in the dog-cart, driven by her husband.

This was the clipping season, and in addition to selling their goods the Kennedys bought, or at least obtained, great quantities of smelly 'clarts' – soiled wool or broken fleeces from the clippings which were too dirty to pack among the clean fleeces. Though glad to be rid of this smelly product of shearing, the herds were often rewarded in kind. Some farmers were so glad to have someone to clean up round the clipping stools that the Kennedys got the clarts for nothing.

Back at their camp they submerged the dirty wool in the nearby running water and washed it thoroughly. The wool, now rid of its unpleasant smell, was spread out on the bank to dry. Once dry, it became white and fleecy and was packed in clean bags ready for sale as first-class wool. For more than half a century the Kennedys rendered a popular service and their caravan, white tent and dog-cart were accepted as part of the rural scene.

Frankie carried on the trade for a few years after his parents retired. He was now married to a very good-looking, dark-skinned, dark-eyed girl. Once they had a family, they gave up the caravan and took over premises in Lochmaben where they bought and sold furniture and antiques. We visited them once only, for something seemed different and their sedentary life seemed to have changed them completely.

A traveller of a different kind turned up at Tweedsmuir annually. Known as the 'grinder', he travelled much of the country with a beautiful little white stallion pony pulling a brightly painted grinding apparatus on wheels. This was used to sharpen axes, shears, knives and anything else that required a sharp edge. It was foot-operated so that he had his hands free to hold the item which was being sharpened. His skill was usually in demand with us and he often stayed overnight, taking good care of his equine companion. He greatly enjoyed his large bowl of porridge and Jersey milk in the morning. He continued his travels for many years but had a very sad end and was found dead one morning after a bout of drinking.

Until the First World War and for some years beyond, our main roads in the valley were surfaced with stone bonded with wet clayey soil. Even though the traffic consisted almost entirely of horse-drawn vehicles, these roads required constant care and upkeep to prevent the formation of deep ruts and potholes. The side roads were merely cart tracks with metalled wheel tracks and grass strips growing in between.

The stone for these roads came from quarries which are still visible. One can be seen above Glenveg and another near Glenbreck. The stone, in blocks which could be handled by one man, was carted to small bays at strategic points along the road. Here it would be reduced to road metal by the stone knapper.

Our local stone knapper was Geordie Bell who lodged with friends near Mossfennan when working in the Tweed area. Early in life he had broken a leg which, through inadequate treatment, had become not only bent but shorter than the other. In spite of this gammy leg Geordie cycled to work daily, mounting his bike from a suitable bank

Geordie Bell's road-making successors in Tweedsmuir.
(*Above*) Steam traction engine.
(*Below*) Roadmen.

or using a back step on the rear wheel. His hammers, with long, slender shafts, were tied along the top bar, his coat to the handlebars, and a bag was slung over his shoulders.

He usually worked sitting on a leather pad with one leg stretched out in front. It was a revelation to see him take a large rough block of stone, turn it to see the grain and then with one seemingly effortless blow from a comparatively small hammer, split the grey whinstone into two or three pieces. These he quickly reduced into 2-inch road metal using a smaller tool. To protect his eyes he wore large convex goggles made of wire gauze.

Curious children on their way to and from school would stop to watch, but as soon as Geordie noticed them he would stop working and only start again once they had moved on. If one approached quietly and unseen and remained quite still, the deft, toil-worn hands could be watched turning and holding each piece in place and, with rhythmic strokes of the hammer, reducing them in size with great precision. Behind him the stone was built into a neat pile with sides at 45 degrees and a level top. When it was finished, the road foreman came with his measure and yardstick and calculated the amount of road metal and the payment due to Geordie. As he always had several heaps to his credit, this usually allowed him to take a short holiday and enjoy a drinking spree.

Eventually a huge mobile crushing machine came into use, drawn and driven by a powerful steam traction engine. The stone still had to be quarried and reduced to handling size but the work of the human stone breaker was no longer required, so Geordie and his brother craftsmen disappeared from the roadside scene.

The work of stone dykers and masons over the years is evident throughout the valley. I remember one in particular, John Dickson, when he was very old and rather bent. Bicycles had come almost too late for him and I would see him on his tricycle toiling up the inclines and wheeling the machine awkwardly up the steeper slopes. Although his progress was slow and pedalling was tiring, he always maintained it was better and faster than the walking he had to do as a young man when his work included stone dyking. When the shepherd's cottage at Gameshope was built, he walked there from Biggar following the track through the hill to the Tweed road at the Logan.

He once told me of a time of great hardship during the life of either his father or grandfather. A team of dykers was then building walls on Mossfennan. Payment was around two pence a yard with the provision of food. This was mainly porridge, but because the local oat crop had failed, some other grain, brought in from England, was used. The dykers did not like this porridge (which was probably made from wheat) but, as there was nothing else, they just had to get used to it.

He described the building of walls where the river flooded over the fields, using large stones and leaving plenty of room for the flood water to pass through. He also described a cairn – the Parritch (porridge)

Cairn – set up on Hearthstane as a landmark for the women who brought their food. A stretch of steep wall on the top of a high ridge there had so much wind striking it that instead of laying the stones flat they built it with thinish slaty stones placed on their edges with as much space as possible between to reduce the resistance to the wind. This was very difficult to accomplish, and to the dykers' credit this section was still functioning until the middle of this century.

The breeding capacity and feeding habits of rabbits could cause considerable damage, particularly to arable crops where almost half the yield could be lost. To keep the numbers down farmers employed professional trappers who knew the ground and habits of the rabbits on every farm. One of the most accomplished trappers in our area was Geordie Carrick who lived in a house called Rowan Bank which he had built on the old coach road.

At the time I knew him he was in his middle years but looked older. He was of average size and build with side whiskers and a reddish beard roughly trimmed. He smoked a 'cutty' (a short-stemmed clay pipe with a steel lid) and wore a tweed hat and jacket with trousers patched at the knees. His heavy, tackety boots served to hammer snares or trap pegs into the ground. His game bag was a most necessary piece of equipment but was not made to the usual gamekeeper's pattern with a net section and game cords. Instead it consisted of one com- partment made of the strongest moleskin (nothing to do with moles) and a wide, strong strap to avoid cutting into the shoulder. In it he could carry some 25 rabbits or 200 snares but only 25 traps. Carrying such heavy loads caused early curvature of the upper spine, a feature noticeable among all trappers, and Geordie became very bent.

Snaring started in the late autumn when the young rabbits were well grown and, if the ground was free of snow, continued until the new year. When snow and hard frost made snaring impossible, he could sometimes use ferrets and purse-nets. Next came trapping time when the rabbits were living in burrows, and he had to know which were occupied and which were vacant. This was the task of his dog, a cross collie-labrador.

A level foundation for the gin trap was made a little way into the burrow and covered with light soil which had been sifted through a small hand riddle. Next came the most skilled part of the operation as the trap had to be set exactly to go off with the pressure of the animal's foot. The trap also had to be invisible and anchored with a peg and chain. As all this had to be done kneeling, Geordie wore

Waggonette at the Crook Inn, *c.* 1910.

leather knee pads. It was a deadly and cruel way of catching rabbits. Sometimes a rabbit escaped, leaving a foot behind, or managed to pull the peg out and escaped taking the peg and trap with it. It was now the job of the dog to find the rabbit, trap and all.

Geordie was seldom seen in the morning, as he examined his snares and traps at daybreak, but in the afternoon one might meet him pushing his bicycle with the whole framework and handlebars hung with neat pairs of rabbits, hung head downwards. The rabbits by this time had been cleaned and coupled, a task that demanded skill and precision. Geordie was an expert. The cleaning had to be done through the smallest aperture possible. The coupling, which involved making a slit in one back leg of each rabbit and threading the other through, had to have the minimum-sized slit to avoid cutting into the meaty part of the limb.

At Broughton railway station piles of hampers lay waiting to carry the furry cargo to Glasgow, which was the only Scottish market, and to other cities in England. The hampers, about 3 feet high, 3 feet long and 2 feet wide, were strong and made for hard use out of woven untreated willow. Inside were two strong bars built lengthwise near the top and on these the pairs of rabbits were hung, ten pairs on each bar. Labelled, with a note inside from the sender, the hampers left on the next available train and were sold by retailers to be on the table the day after Geordie brought them off the hill.

Knife-grinder.

Stone-knapper.

Stone dykers.

Geordie's work was seasonal, and in late spring and summer (months without an 'r') he had alternative employment. This included catching foxes, some freelance gamekeeping, gardening, beekeeping, and helping with the clipping. He was a successful beekeeper at an altitude just under the 'bee line' and dependent entirely on white clover and heather for the honey. He had a unique relationship with his bees and could handle them with the 'reek of his cutty' instead of using a smoker.

When cutting machines came into use toward the end of the nineteenth century, Moudie (mole) men became necessary to the farming industry. Mole hills stood well above ground and in our part of the country contained a fair number of stones and gravel which blunted or broke the cutting blades of the mowing machines. As this caused delays, the moles had to be dealt with by trapping.

Moudie men, like rabbit catchers, at first used bicycles, but as soon as the motorcycle came into use they obtained these with side cars which could hold all their gear. This included spades, game bags, traps and sometimes boards on which to nail the skins. Farmers would pay them an annual retainer but their main living came from selling the moleskins. These were at their best in the winter and early spring. Moles were skinned soon after being killed and the skin, nearly square and measuring only four or five inches, was then nailed to a board to dry. The skins were sold to the fur trade for between 6d and 7d each and were used to make coats, collars, cuffs and trimmings.

In winter the services of the mole catchers, trappers, fencers and dykers were called upon when the roads became impassable with drifts of snow. With wide, bare, treeless spaces stretching on both sides of the road, snow blew in great quantities along the surface and settled in drifts. Where there were walls, the snow settled to their tops and was channeled by the terrain into high ridges. Gangs of workers who came from lower areas to clear the roads were assisted by local mole catchers, rabbit trappers, fencers and dykers and others whose usual work was curtailed because of the snow. Heavy snowfalls often coincided with hard frost, sometimes the whole countryside was smothered in white and even the Tweed was obliterated. Further up the valley the road was only traceable by the snow posts. Talla road would be badly blocked near the dam but the Menzion and Fruid road could usually be cleared with a horse-drawn snow plough.

Until the arrival of buses and coaches, public transport relied on horse-drawn vehicles. However, for a short period at the turn of the century Tweedsmuir inhabitants had an alternative. In 1894 the Edinburgh and District Water Trustees decided to build a new reservoir at Talla to supply water to the Edinburgh area. As the roads were not suitable for carrying the materials needed for this major construction, a railway line was built between Broughton and Talla. The cabin of the train could take five passengers and the public were allowed to make the eight-mile journey between Tweedsmuir and Broughton for a small charge. This means of travel lasted for only a few years while the reservoir and pipeline were being built. Immediately the work was completed, the line was dismantled and the railway link severed.

With the end of the railway a long period ensued when public transport was provided by the horse-drawn vehicles owned by two operators, Ritchie Ross of the Bield and Willie Newbigging of Broughton. Ritchie, who farmed a small acreage, had one horse and two vehicles, a waggonette for good weather and a brougham for wet conditions. The waggonette, a open four-wheeled carriage, could take about half a dozen passengers in the facing side seats and one beside the driver. The brougham was very different. It was completely closed in with side doors and could take only four passengers. It was very old and the inside, which was upholstered in worn leather, had a musty odour which became very evident when the windows were closed and was inclined to remain with the passengers after the journey had ended.

Passengers alighting from the train at Broughton were always relieved if the waggonette was waiting to take them to Tweedsmuir. Ritchie's horses always looked underfed and weakly and at the inclines at Stanhope Brae and Logan the passengers had to get down and walk until the road became flatter. I don't remember Ritchie smoking much but he was known as Reekie Ross and sometimes Auld Reekie.

Willie Newbigging's establishment at Broughton included a waggonette and also a hearse. The waggonette was fairly big with two horses and could take a large number of passengers on longer journeys to places such as West Linton and Peebles. I have a vivid recollection of a trip to Moffat Agricultural Show. As a treat to his employees, Mr Thorburn had hired the big waggonette to carry the families over the Beef Tub to Moffat and back. The journey started quite early, for it took three hours each way. Annan Water was full of mist and a strip of hoar still stretched along the valley. As we neared Moffat, we could see the then famous Hydropathic, outstanding in its red sandstone, rising out of the mist. The next time we saw it it consisted of a burnt out shell, never to be rebuilt.

Like the Hydropathic, the cadgers, moudie men and others I have described have all disappeared from the valley. In their time they gave great service to the inhabitants, and their work and stamina did much to make the hard lives of those days a little easier.

Chapter Eight *Fishing*

The arrival of the fish runs in the headwaters of the Tweed must have been one of the most important events of the year from time immemorial. Before the reservoirs were built, the large streams of Talla and Fruid, called 'waters', flowed through extensive marshes known as 'lakes'. In periods of heavy rainfall the lakes, especially at Talla, acted like large sponges and stored a great mass of water. This afforded long periods of high water sufficient to allow salmon and sea trout to ascend in great numbers. In Talla Lakes the dark waters of one pool, fringed with overhanging saughs, were reputed to harbour salmon all the year round.

Tales abound of the enormous runs of both sea trout and salmon and how they were used. So many arrived at one time that only a small proportion could be used immediately. The remainder were 'reested' - cleaned and split, then salted and hung near the peat fire to dry. They were then hung, like bacon, from the 'kipples' (rafters). This source of good food was much appreciated in the winter months, especially in areas where cultivation was difficult.

One tale, dating from the 1870s, is of a huge early run of sea trout in Talla (before the dam) when groups of young shepherds killed so many that they could not take them all away. The remainder, left in a sheep shed, were never collected and the putrifying fish were eventually discovered by the head shepherd. When one of the participants, who was made to clear up the mess, recounted the incident, he added the comment that it had taught him the virtue of moderation at all times, 'even at the fishing'.

Sometimes the runs of fish were late in reaching the headwaters and on one occasion, when the long-awaited shoals arrived on a Sunday, the Minister at that time had great difficulty in restraining his congregation until midnight.

On another occasion news came that the Kingledores Burn was packed with fish, and an expedition from Broughton set out at night with a cart. As the owner, Mr Stewart, was very much against the taking of salmon, ropes were wound round the iron-shod wheels of the cart to deaden the noise when it passed his house. The expedition was successful and the fish were duly shared throughout the village.

Using the leister.

Usually the first runs were of sea trout followed by a run of red fish, followed by a final run in January of smaller blue 'buttoners'. These were preferred to the others as they were always finer-fleshed and of a size suitable for 'reesting'. Owners of parts of the river had established a close season, and laws were passed decreeing how and when salmon could be caught. Nevertheless ancient methods of killing salmon were still used all the way up the river.

Cleiks (iron hooks), leisters (pronged spears) and dregs were the weapons used to get fish for domestic use but fish traps and nets were used lower down the river to catch large numbers for sale. Night fishing was generally practised in the upper half of the river. Light was provided by a blazing torch held high over the water. This had the effect of showing up the shining fish and at the same time dazzling and blinding them.

The cleik was simply a large hook fixed to a stick of variable length. Leisters were of two sorts. One was used for spearing fish within reach of the very long 12–15 foot shaft. After spearing the fish was pressed hard on the bottom of the river or burn and held against the current to prevent the flow of water aiding its escape.

The other type of leister was slightly different. It had a shorter shaft with a cord attached which was used by throwing like a harpoon. 'Clodding' was the term used for throwing a leister, and a good clodder could reach fish 15 to 20 yards away. The clodding leister had to be

Talla Valley before the Reservoir, looking west.

Talla Valley before the Reservoir, looking east.

carefully made and balanced. Usually it was made with 4 prongs (though originally with 5) which were graduated in length. As these instruments were made by local blacksmiths, they varied slightly in shape, in the 'rake' of the prongs and in the 'watters' or barbs on the prongs. Certain smiths became renowned for their skill in making superior examples.

The clodding leister could be thrown double-handed, and when the target was hit the shaft carried right over, like a well-tossed caber. The current would than carry the end of the shank downstream, holding the fish against the flow and doubly ensuring it did not escape when pulled in by the rope. If the clod was not so perfect and the shaft fell back, there was the likelihood that the leister would be pulled out of the fish.

Success with the leister depended on an accurate throw which struck the fish forward through the head. If struck too far back, fish could escape, often with horrible tears, only to perish later especially if the backbone had been damaged. Unless the fish was hit by a head shot, it was inevitable that deep penetration of the barbed prongs resulted in wasted meat.

Dregs consisted of three hooks tied together to make a treble at the end of a long line with a lead weight to sink it. Dregging, or sniggling, took a great deal of skill and accuracy and some people became very expert. One of these was 'Stumpy' Robb from Broughton who had only one leg and used crutches. He had one serious disadvantage as he could not run away, yet he avoided arrest because his hooks were easily concealed.

Some illegal fishing of trout occurred in summer with the use of a nocturnal device known as an otter. This was simply a shaped piece of wood about one inch thick with a hoop of wire on one side. A long line attached to the hoop controlled the angle of the device in the stream and it could be guided anywhere. On still water the operator had to move along the bank to give it a pull on the water, like flying a kite in the air. When trailing a long line of night flies it was reputed to be deadly.

The building of the Talla dam and reservoir at the turn of the twentieth century drastically changed the situation for fish and fishing. In the first winters following the completion of the work, the salmon ascending Talla, hoping to reach the pools and spawning gravels, filled the stretch below the overflow so thickly that it was said you could walk across their backs dry-shod. This continued for a few years but with the fish numbers decreasing. Though some continued to spawn in the lower parts of Talla, when the compensation water was later reduced, spawning was cut to almost nil.

Some small fish were now ascending Fruid in summer (as they had earlier done in Talla) and found sanctuary in the dark pools of the lakes until their spawning period in early October. The lower Tweed at this time was a good springer water and this may be the explanation of the Fruid early spawners. Not all these fish were small, though most ranged from 4–6 lbs and were sometimes joined by sea trout in varying numbers.

A variety of sea trout, called 'Dum Sea Trout' by old-timers, which came in regular runs in the nineteenth century, still arrived in small numbers and often with running salmon. They were stocky, thickset fish with rich creamy flesh and in the water showed along the back a brownish terracotta colour with a cream-coloured belly.

With the River Tweed close to my home and the Hearthstane Burn nearby it wasn't surprising that I became addicted to fishing at an early age. The Hearthstane Bridge (we called it the 'Brig') crossed the Tweed opposite our cottage at right angles to the main road and afforded a perfect platform for watching the activities of the fish. They regularly chose the gravelly stretch where the bridge was situated to

Talla Reservoir.

make their redds (spawn). Even when the water level was too high for spawning we could see fish, usually in pairs, making their way up-stream. This was only possible because we were looking straight down on them with the least amount of water to see through.

To us small children the Brig was magic. In lowish water one only needed to climb up and hang over the upstream rail, look down through the clear rippling water at the gravel below and, in a split second, one seemed to be off upstream, bridge and all. When Jim and I were very small the top rail was out of reach but we got the same sensation when we poked our heads through the lower cross-rail. There was a big pool, the Wisdom Pool, with rocky sides at a bend about a quarter of a mile upstream. We never reached it in our game, for a casual glance at the bank brought us immediately back to our starting point and reality.

The wide gravel bed on the Hearthstane side of the river below the Brig became a favourite playground. Jim and I made pools at the edge of the gravel which were near enough to fill up with water. Here we put small minnows about two inches long, caught by hand, and small parr which I had caught by fishing. The worms and flies we fed them were hardly ever eaten but tiny little newly hatched, almost transparent 'pinheads' appeared from nowhere. We called them pinheads because of their big heads and small bodies.

Some burns attracted numbers of sea trout but the Hearthstane Burn always had so much gravel at the mouth that it impeded fish trying to ascend. Jim and I moved the obstructing gravel and formed a single channel which turned downstream along with the river water. Thus the fish coming up during the night followed naturally up the flow into the burn. Though their progress was eventually stopped by high waterfalls, they would stay until daybreak. In this way we got sea trout but seldom a decent-sized salmon.

Carlowes Bridge (the 'Linn Brig'), the main stone bridge which crosses the Tweed, was also a favourite spot from which to watch fish. The bridge spans the gorge below two waterfalls and at the beginning of the twentieth century the water of the lower fall dropped several feet in a solid spout into a foaming whirlpool. This required a clear leap by ascending fish and the spectacle attracted many observers, especially the children from the nearby school. We spent much time watching, entranced by the struggles, the frequent failures and, of course, the successes of the finny denizens of the then mighty Tweed. During heavy floods the flow covered much of the rock walls and the fish did not require to show themselves, and in low water no fish were travelling at all.

The only way we could see into the deep Linn Pool was to hold out a cap and look down its shadow, like the pearl fishers of the Tay. Even then fish lying close under the overhanging rock were too far underneath to be seen. If one watched until the fish breathed out, bubbles could be seem coming from the depths of the river. In this way we could make a guess at the number of fish as well as their size.

On one side of the bridge there is a narrow ledge running across from side to side, about four feet above the rushing water and pro-truding rocks. Only the surefooted could reach this ledge and it certainly wasn't for the fainthearted. One day we schoolchildren were watching the leaping salmon from the top of the bridge when one large fish cleared the fall in a flying leap, but instead of keeping straight up towards the top fall he seemed to turn towards an eddy where he could be reached by treble hooks and handline. It took me no time to get over a set of steps and down over the rocks, and there the waving tail showed the position of the fish. But just then came the call from the watchers on the bridge that the bailiffs were coming on their bikes. There was no time to lose and nowhere to go except the ledge under the bridge, and there I sat for what seemed an eternity. Fortunately the bailiffs stayed on the bridge for only a few minutes before moving on. Then a voice from overhead called that the coast was clear and I

Andrew Lorimer, fisherman.

could emerge just in time for the bell ringing the end of the dinner hour.

As well as trout and salmon the deep waters by Carlowes Bridge suited ordinary adult eels in summer. In midsummer an unusual phenomenon could generally be witnessed. This was the arrival of the young elvers (eels) from the far-off Sargasso Sea. None were more than half the thickness of a pencil and they swarmed up the moist steep stone-holding on among pieces of growing moss or any slight cleft. Evidently the dropping water of the fall prevented them from following the main course. There seemed no hope that they would get over the obstacles they were attempting, yet after a day or two there were few still to be seen. They had found some way onwards, for there were always eels well above Tweedsmuir.

During the 1914–18 war scarcity of food increased as the war progressed, aggravated by the success of the Greman U-boats in sinking ships bringing in products that people had come to depend upon. This wartime scarcity reawakened the hereditary fishing urge, and the old skills were revived as the rusty leisters and cleiks were retrieved from their hiding places and refurbished. It was almost an unwritten obligation for menfolk to provide fish for use and to store.

The newly formed Tweed Commission employed watchers (baillies) to patrol the river but, although they made the odd arrest of people getting 'one for the pot', they couldn't be everywhere at once. Further down the river organised poaching unfortunately became a way of life for many and a huge trade was carried on using the railway system.

Fish were not caught in our own case for selling but always for using or giving away. Sometimes a few land workers near the roads did a bit of small-scale poaching. No one ever thought of using nets though we heard of them being used by gangs lower down the river. Once or twice gangs raided our upper waters at night using a blazing 'doosie' to illuminate the whole river. The flaming torch was held high overhead, and two or three poachers using leisters took the whole water in front of them. Quite quickly the spectacular display moved downstream with the reflection overhead of their light indicating their course down the valley. We seldom heard of these large gangs being caught, even though they made little attempt at concealment.

I have described elsewhere how Jim and I landed three large salmon one night using our lamp and an old leister and the trouble it got us into with our parents. My experiences as a 'clodder' were equally dramatic. One morning on my way to school I made a detour to look into the river at my favourite stream, the Bield Scaur. I was surprised to find Jimmy Brown gazing across the fast-running stream. He had been the best clodder in Tweed but his sight was failing, and although he had seen a fish earlier, he couldn't now locate it. I could see it clearly and explained that it was a long way out in the middle. He told me he needed a fish as he had friends coming from Glasgow at the weekend and added as an afterthought, 'Can ye clod laddie?' The laddie was keen enough to try. I was instructed to keep the fish under observation while he went for his leister, which I learned later he often kept hidden in a field drain pipe nearby.

In a few minutes he was back with the best weapon I have ever seen. The prongs were shining, evidently sandpapered, the barbs not too big and the points filed sharp. The proportions were perfect and the shank quite thin, rounded and painted. Instead of a rope a stiffish cord was attached, so there was little or no drag on its flight. This was no ordinary leister. This was indeed the 'Excalibur' of all leisters. Old Jimmy held the cord and I threw with all my might. The leister impaled the fish perfectly, the shaft continued over like a well-tossed caber and Jimmy drew in the fish. 'Aye laddie, ye can clod, but dinna let on' was my reward and we kept our secret. I had attained one of my great ambitions. I was now a 'clodder' by old Jimmy's standards. I hurried off to arrive just in time for school.

Jimmy Brown died a few years later and 'Excalibur' was inherited by his son. I had, however, carried a pattern of it in my mind and eventually managed to have a near replica made of it in, of all places, Colville's Ironworks in Motherwell. During a talk with an ironworker who was a real fisherman, I told him about 'Excalibur' and he immediately volunteered to make a perfect copy if I could give him a drawing. Evidently a great deal of steel sheeting some ¼-inch thick lay about in odd shapes left over as waste. My leister was newly cut from one of these oddments, rounded and smoothed to perfection. I put it in a joiner-made shaft and, though perhaps a little heavier, it behaved very much like old Jimmy's.

In the next few years my copy of Jimmy Brown's leister performed with deadly, almost too deadly, accuracy. My clodding career, however, ended quite abruptly when one day some friends from Edinburgh went with me to see the fish. Further downstream in some deeper water I could see two blue shapes behind a large sunken boulder. They were rising and falling, sometimes one rising near the surface and then the other. Only the thin line down their backs was visable because the silvery scales on their sides reflected the surroundings exactly. This was the fish dance, part of the mating ritual, which few people have seen and few would even notice.

I went to get my leister and was surprised to find the fish still there when I returned. I made a long clod (throw) when one was near the surface, but the other must have been rising at the same time. Both were killed instantly and I drew in a pair of shining spring salmon of around 12lbs each. It was a fluke of course, but the over-success and the sight of the two silvery beauties has haunted me ever since. Stricken with a strong feeling of remorse, I vowed I would never use a leister again. From that day I never handled a leister and the spell of Excalibur gradually faded except as a memory associated with old Jimmy Brown and his precious accolade 'Ye can clod'.

When my brother was shepherd at Badlieu, I enjoyed going there to fish. A previous young shepherd had left an old fishing rod behind which I was allowed to use, at first only in the burn. To begin with the rod was too heavy for me and I needed both hands to hold it over the water. Fortunately there were so many fish, mainly parr, swarming everywhere that, using worms on a single hook you couldn't help catching them.

Back at Hearthstane I was fishing at every opportunity though still with bait. One day when I was fishing on the Tweed, a visitor staying at Glenveg saw me. This was Jean Lang, author and historian, the sister of Andrew Lang the poet and essayist. Like her brother she was a keen angler and often fished on Talla and occasionally on Tweed. Fly fishing had become the fashion by this time, and when her holiday ended she gave my mother an envelope addressed to me. Inside was a smaller transparent envelope, tightly sealed, but showing a cast of bright loch flies, the standard Talla selection, Butcher, Peter Ross and Greenwell's Glory. The instructions were to use them when I was older and had more experience. Now and then I had a peep at my very own gaudy lures and held them up to the light so I could see the famous red loop, the guarantee of Martin's quality. Until I was allowed to use them they were never opened and were kept safely with some other treasures high up on the big kitchen dresser.

At this time two young people, known to me as John and Ann, came for a week or so each summer and camped with Mr Thorburn's permission a short distance up the burn. They got milk, eggs, scones and butter from us and I joined some of their fishing expeditions. I was always sad to see them go. The war was now on and the struggle was becomimg more intense when late one day they arrived and pitched their tent nearer than before. I did not see them and they left quite early the next morning, leaving with my mother their 9-foot Greenheart fly rod to give to me. John was leaving for active service and, although I didn't understand it at the time, they were saving me and themselves a sad farewell, for they never returned. Neither would have come without the other to a scene of such happiness. I now had the famous flies and a good rod though I had to wait some time before being allowed to use it.

One day when we schoolchildren were wading barefoot below the pool at Carlowes Bridge in the sandy gravel thrown up behind the rocks, a thread-like line twined round my ankles. On getting hold of it I found it came from much deeper water. It seemed never-ending but eventually a fishing reel appeared dragging along the gravel. It was a first-class Hardy and, once the sand was cleaned out and the action well oiled, I had a really good reel with a long tapered line. Someone had been fishing in the deep Linn Pool between the rocks, had fallen in and had lost both rod and line but was lucky to get out alive. No one claimed the reel and it fitted the Greenheart to perfection. I now had my Martin's red loop, John's rod and a perfect reel. My aspiration was now to be allowed to fish the preserved waters of Talla.

The wished-for opportunity came quite unexpectedly. The supervisor at Talla required roe from the Loch Leven stock in the loch for his hatchery. Some of the adult employees had been unsuccessful and his son, Jock, suggested that I might be able to help. We went off with a landing net and a pail and instructions to return with about half a pail of spawn. We found hen fish in runnels and small burns at the head of the loch and captured them under the banks, netting them in the shallow streams where some were already spawning. Soon we had the pail half full and returned highly pleased with ourselves. The last request now materialised and I was given permission to fish Talla in the evenings.

It wasn't until the following summer that I was able to fish on Talla. How often it happens that great expectations crumble into anticlimax. The flies did their part quite well but the fish were nearly all under the limit for size and much easier to land than anticipated. Though indulging occasionally in still water fishing, I cannot help rating it far below the thrill of fast water, rock and tree hazards and fighting quarry on tackle of breaking strain well below that of the fish. Looking back on Jean Lang's cast of flies, John's Greenheart fly rod, the line and reel from the Linn Pool and finally the unexpected privilege of fishing Talla, it looked as though the fates were pushing me into a fishing career.

During the Glasgow Fair holidays a number of miners and steel-workers came up Tweed, some cycling and some walking from Broughton railway station. They brought with them the minimum of camping equipment (their tents were very small), but they always had big fishing baskets and spliced rods. Fishing on this part of the Tweed was free and on most of the burns except, of course, on Talla.

These men often fished all night if the conditions were right and most fished with horsehair casts and home-tied flies. Sometimes they used a little brown fly with upright wings, known as the 'Wren's tail'. Their casts were made of single hairs joined by a special sliding knot which made changing flies a quick and easy operation. As hair had a comparatively low breaking point, trout had to be treated very gently. The fact that it yielded slightly helped, and their spliced rods were always tapered so finely that they were extremely whippy. The droppers stuck out at right angles from the cast because the hairs, though hollow, were slightly stiff. Skilful anglers could cast gently on to overhanging branches, rocks or overhanging grassy or rushy banks and shake their flies into the water below without entanglement.

The miners' and steelworkers' fishing holidays, though often marred by weather conditions, were to many of them the highlight of the year, and they must have spent much time preparing their gear. I learned 'real' fishing from these men but most of all from Jimmy Kerr. He was one of a family of three boys, all of whom followed their father down the pits. When war broke out they all volunteered but all were so affected by miner's lung that they were eventually discharged. One returned to mining, one became a pig farmer and Jimmy, whom I knew best, became a bricklayer relining the still-hot kilns used in smelting. All died quite young but Jimmy passed on his fishing and fly-tying skills to me. One skill that I failed to acquire was his expertise as a piper. Though I started on the chanter, I always seemed to have other irons in the fire.

These miners usually got their horsehair from white ponies that dragged the 'hutches' (baskets for carrying coal) in the mines. The hair had to be as long as possible, to have come from a young male pony and be a fairly transparent white. Sometimes they even made horsehair lines but these didn't last long as the ends of the hair tended to stick out and wear off on the rungs of the rod.

There were two particular incidents, one involving a hair line and the other a hair cast which have stayed in my memory. One early summer I was fishing horsehair flies as usual but was trying out a 6-ply horsehair line. As I approached a rock pool well above Tweedsmuir, I realised there were salmon there and hurriedly took off the hair cast and substituted strongish gut. My only suitable salmon hook was a small double silver doctor and with this I hooked a fish. The rocks were steep and I had to get the little salmon (it turned out to be under 4lbs) down over the tail of the pool. Every time we got near the tail he saw me and turned back up the pool, each time rubbing the line hard against the rocks. When he eventually left the pool, he made the mistake of following a diminishing runnel and was scooped out. This was just in time, for where the line had been running through the tip of the rod only one hair was left on the line.

The other incident occurred on a long flat pool above Hearthstane where I had seen at dusk the V-shaped ripple of a biggish trout. I set out the next morning and approached the lower gravelly side cautiously and made my first cast in the rippling water at the head of the pool. The cast had hardly landed when, to my disgust, a small parr hooked itself on one of the flies. To avoid disturbance, as this was where the 'big one' should be, I slackened the line to let the little thing drift along without splashing so I could deal with it quietly. Halfway down the stream a head broke the surface, the parr disappeared and the fish was securely hooked. How the hook transferred itself to the bigger fish I still do not know. Eventually I landed him further down-stream where hand and foot work plus landing net all contributed to his capture. To my great disappointment it weighed just over 1¼lbs but there was some consolation as the breaking point of the hair tackle could only have been ½lb or thereabouts. To a teenage beginner these two incidents remained among the most important and encouraging events in a whole lifetime on the riverside.

By now I had become a lone operator on most fishing expeditions for, without distractions, I could be more successful. I often found myself fishing well after the light had faded, for then the large moths and flies came on the water and larger trout fed on them. My expeditions gradually took me further afield, and I can always remember crossing from one burn to another up Fruid and suddenly finding I had intruded on the privacy of a large, dark-grey billy goat. His rough coat, grey beard and long black horns gave him a very frightening appearance and I was much relieved when, after a long confrontation, he retreated along the rocky hill face.

On another occasion I encountered a fox carrying a grouse. It was almost dark and he passed no great distance away from me without knowing I was there. While standing dead still, a strange feeling crept over me. It was a mixture of excitement, a kind of fear, tenseness – something instinctive and primitive. I am quite sure other people have experienced this too for I have seen reynard escape his foes as though he had put them under a spell.

Fishing late, even long after the fall of darkness, there were eerie sounds and mysterious changes in the continuous song of the running waters. No wonder our forefathers believed in water sprites and kelpies. At one point up Tweed a distinct rumbling sound seemed to suggest a living source somewhere below the surface ready to emerge and confront the unwary. It came from a great boulder on the bottom where air and an errant current met and built a miniature whirlpool which at intervals rose rumbling to the surface.

The ultimate output of fish on a river depends entirely on the spawning success and survival of fry to adulthood. Few fish come from the reaches in which they are caught and most originate in the headwaters where there is no salmon fishing and hardly any trout fishing. While the 'take' reaches are managed with much assiduity, the upper reaches which provide a large proportion of the natural stock are largely ignored.

The situation on the Tweed has been aggravated by the appropriation of all the main spawning streams to provide water for Edinburgh and the surrounding area. The building of Talla dam and reservoir removed one of the main spawning streams but left the waters of Fruid untouched until the second dam and reservoir were built there in the 1960s.

Fruid Lakes, similar to Talla but with less water, did not attract many fish because of a drainage system introduced to get hay from the bogs. When the drainage system was discontinued, larger pools formed and summer fish (mainly small gravid hens) could be counted in the dark pools by September. Though some fell prey to the otters which always bred there, most succeeded in spawning, usually in late September. In summer so many parr filled the water that trout fishing became impossible.

As an example of fish numbers in Fruid, about 1947 in late September or early October there were 25 fish trapped in one pool while the overhanging banks further up were packed with part-hidden fish with their tails exposed, adding perhaps another score. Some were badly scarred, with damaged fins and tails from the attentions of a family of young otters. A week later the otters had killed a few and seriously hurt others but a rise in the water level the following week allowed them to scatter and spawn. The charts relating to spring salmon show a decline which may be connected with the loss of Fruid in the late 1960s when the dam and reservoir were constructed.

The dams at Talla and Fruid could have been provided with fish

Tweedsmuir Bridge.

passes but no one appears to have been interested enough to draw the attention of the authorities to this possibility. Worse still, where a stream is dammed the stretch below the dam loses its productivity. Good spawning gravel requires continual renewal from moving material, scoured and clean, which each year fills up the redds of the previous year to the original level of the stream bed. In my own experience it has been noticeable that year after year in good gravels the same redds have been dug right down to the larger stones which form the lower layer of the bed. The gravel below a dam receives no freshly scoured replacement and not enough disturbance to keep it open and moveable. The bed then becomes too firm for fish to dig properly and too dense to give passage to the hatching elvins when they start to move in early spring.

The damming of Talla also affected the large number of eels which were in the Lakes. When the dam was constructed, no others could get over the huge barrier to join them. When, during floods, some of the special trout, which had been reared by John Watt the supervisor, escaped all the way down to Tweed, a small mesh barrier was fitted to keep the trout in the loch. The result was that eels above these screens were stopped when they tried to migrate back to breed in the Sargasso Sea. These eels were now mature, up to 3 or 4 feet in length and as thick as a man's arm.

Although this happened nearly ten years after the completion of the dam, these eels had only then reached full spawning condition and were plump and silvery and made very good eating. The number of eels gradually diminished over the years, and eventually there were none left in the loch. When Fruid, Menzion, Hawkshaw and Fingland were dammed in the 1960s, eels lost more of their territory, though they can still be found in some upper waters. Here they have become a favourite food for mink and herons. Mink often feed their young with eels and carry them over long distances.

Brown trout spawn much further up the burns than either sea trout or salmon. In Upper Tweed above Drumelzier the burns from the east are all more or less impassable for many fish right up to Talla. The remaining really good waters are either dammed or diverted into the reservoirs at Talla and Fruid right up to the head of the Tweed where even Glencraigs has an obstructive waterfall.

Three of these burns, Polmood, Hearthstane and Glenriskie, are unique in that some short distance from their junction with Tweed high waterfalls bar the passage of spawners of any kind. Above these

4.1 Neidpath Castle

4.2 March Riders below Neidpath Castle

4.3 Holylee to Elibank

4.4 The Eildons

4.5 Morning View from Glentress Forest

4.6 Manor Bridge

4.7 Fruid Water before the Reservoir

4.8 The Riggs with Bell Shaw at the Burn

falls indigenous trout with very individual markings occur. These streams do not contribute much to the river stock except perhaps a few sea trout from the short stretches at their mouths. All, however, have been partly forested, which may reduce fish activity both above and below the falls.

Hearthstane Burn, which is fed by pure spring water and runs open to the sky, was inhabited by clear, shiny trout with bright markings which resembled those of parr. In its tributory, Glenheurie, which runs in shaded conditions, there were trout with dark markings and large red spots.

Most of the other tributaries have been affected by forestry work undertaken since the Second World War. This at times has caused serious dimunition and sometimes elimination of fish in the headwaters. Though some improvement has followed the stabilisation of the ploughing, too much very fine sediment from the peatlands still settles in the upper spawning grounds.

The loss of fish to predators, often erroneously believed to be negligible, is now complicated by the spread of mink and goosanders. Mink can winter in remote burns where they feed on spent fish which lie dormant for much of the winter under banks and stones. Goosanders, now protected birds, were practically unknown before 1930. In the late 1920s they occasionally came into the upper waters and were largely dealt with by the gamekeepers of the district.

Nesting in the Tweed catchment was first recorded in 1933 or 1934. They first bred in Upper Tweed in 1939 when no fewer than 16 were seen on Talla reservoir – and dealt with. During the war years that followed, even though the keepers had all gone, the goosanders were not allowed to increase, and until the 1950s they were held in control. The pest officer, T. Sked, often visited Talla to shoot duck flighting off at dusk or in the early morning. Goosanders spending the night on the reservoir came off and on at the same times but in opposite directions, and he was responsible for keeping the population well under control for many years.

With the Fruid reservoir as an additional sanctuary in the late 1960s many goosander broods escaped and the annual autumn count on Talla and Fruid reached around one hundred. Hatched early in April and May, each bird by autumn had already consumed at least 1,000 young fish. Young birds can eat their own weight of fish daily and sometimes so gorge themselves that, if disturbed, they have to disgorge in order to escape.

In these narrow upper waters the stock of parr is soon depleted, and lately the goosanders have started to visit smaller tributaries which by midsummer they can almost clear. Often those fish which do escape, instead of having the usual clear colourings, are dark-skinned from living under banks and stones. I am sure a case could be made for the removal of goosanders from the protected list by re-examining the grounds on which they were included.

Looking back on a fairly long life, I realise that much of my youth could have been better used. My consuming interest in fishing and the natural world took me on long excursions to wild and desolate places. I had no desire for company, as successful angling requires complete concentration on the task in hand. Although I never made a career of fishing, it has been one of the greatest pleasures of my life, and I am only sorry that I have witnessed the gradual decline of the fish stocks in the once mighty Tweed.

Chapter Nine   *Nature Notes*

The Upper Tweed Valley was a wonderful place for children who, like me, were interested in the natural world. I was fortunate to grow up at a time when the valley was without its present large tracts of forestry and when the young could wander without fear or constraint. Even the walk to school each day provided endless interest with the great variety of wildlife in and beside the river and nearby burns. After school and in holiday time I was able to explore further afield and developed my great love of the surrounding countryside and the creatures that inhabit it.

As boys we were always interested in birds' nests and eggs but not through mere curiosity. Many kinds of eggs were edible but not easily obtainable and all, of course, had to be fresh. The most saleable were those of the peewit (plover) which, in the years before the First World War and a few years later, were gathered in large numbers by the ploughmen and landworkers.

Fields were ploughed in winter and cultivated fairly late in spring and the peewits, having wintered on southern coasts, only returned just before the start of cultivation. The plough furrows made ideal sites as the peewits wanted their nests, which were mere hollows, to be high and dry. They invariably laid four eggs, so the nests had to be visited almost daily to be sure of taking only fresh eggs. When seeding started and the drills were levelled, the birds soon made new nests on the newly sown land. Their next eggs were reared in safety and there was no decline in the peewit numbers. In some areas the eggs were collected at railway stations and sent to London in specially made wooden boxes with partitions to keep them safe.

Unfortunately this state of affairs could not continue, and shortly after the end of the First World War egg collecting became unlawful except before certain dates. These dates were fixed without taking account of the weather, the seasons or the differences in climate between districts. The result was that birds' nests containing half-hatched eggs (which before would have been lifted fresh) were destroyed in the course of cultivation and few young were hatched. Modern methods of cultivation have completed this decline except for the small number of peewits which nest on moors or grassland.

Curlew and wild duck eggs were also popular. If a wild duck clutch was regularly gathered, the duck continued to lay, thus producing double the number of eggs. Wild duck sometimes even laid in nests used by domestic fowls. At Badlieu one spring a wild duck laid daily in the bedding in the unused pig sty which she shared with one of the ordinary farm ducks.

Opposite Hearthstane a very steep hill face was honeycombed with rabbit burrows which in spring were always taken over by jackdaws. The takeover was quite methodical: while the rabbits were feeding, the jackdaws occupied the burrows, so when the rabbits returned they faced the strong beaks of the jackdaws at every entrance. A peck or two with tufts of fur flying soon gave the birds unopposed possession.

As this colony of jackdaws tended to grow too numerous with serious effects on farm crops, Jim and I were deputed to keep them in control by taking their eggs. The nests, a foot or more from the entrance of the burrow, were solidly built of twigs and heather stems (birns) interwoven with wool and grass or anything that the birds could find. Paper, like torn-up letters, bits of cloth, fragments of china or tin, and pieces of string could all be found in the nests. It was difficult to get a hand into these nests to remove the eggs as they were built so tightly into the tunnels.

Sometimes we had to use a walking stick with a turned handle or a shank with a strong metal hook attached and pull out the nests whose eggs we could not remove by hand. The eggs from the incomplete clutches were taken home, and next morning we had jackdaw egg omelettes for breakfast. By these means, although some eggs always hatched, the jackdaw numbers were controlled.

In addition to nests of edible eggs we always knew a great number of others. On buildings there were martins, swallows and house sparrows. Tree sparrows nested on spruces around the farm. Sandpipers, redshanks, dippers and wagtails nested on the walls; blackbirds, hedge sparrows, chaffinches, mistle thrush and pigeons on low bushes and trees; owls, kestrels, occasionally merlins and sparrowhawks in the woods. In young plantations there were bullfinches and goldcrests with tiny warblers whose names we didn't know. Game birds, partridge, grouse and black game were plentiful, and there were even a few wild pheasants. Herons had local colonies too but the arch enemy of all was the carrion (hoodie) crow. How many of this large variety can be found today?

On the hills we knew nests which our betters did not wish us to visit as often as we wanted. It was always vexing to discover that a nest we had found had later been completely destroyed by the ever-watchful hoodies (carrion crows). When no eggs or shells were left, we knew they had been carried off to feed their own young. If broken with sticky remnants and nearby scattered feathers, we presumed that a fox had caught the hen bird on the nest. If the shells were in halves and some fitted neatly together we knew that the chicks had hatched safely. Black game were very vulnerable. Wild duck nested far away up the hill burns and often far from water. They had a method of foiling the crows by covering their eggs with a mixture of down and grass whenever they left the nest.

One year a hoodie nest was missed in a wood by gamekeepers. We found this nest but the young were almost ready to fly. At a nearby vantage point near a spring we saw where the parent birds had sucked the eggs of their victims and carried the contents to feed their own brood. The ground all round was littered with empty shells, some with only a small hole in the side but otherwise complete. We counted well over a hundred eggs. Most were of grouse but black game, peewits, partridge, wild duck and even golden plover were among them. That, of course, did not give a complete picture of the destructive capacity of the hoodies as later their food would include the young of the ground nesters as well.

A rather rare nest, that of a merlin, was to be found most years, though not regularly, in Glenheurie, a picturesque, narrow ravine between the rig of that name and the Crooked Bank. The scattered birks (birch) and rowans all had old hoodie nests which the merlin sometimes used. Once it nested on the ground in heather on the very edge of the overhanging top of a big red scaur. The round, red, slightly marled eggs, a little like those of the kestrel with which they sometimes competed, were a great attraction. Although we occasionally took one from a clutch, the birds did not abandon their nest as other species might have done.

The small heronry in Hog Hill Wood fascinated us. The wood, mainly of mature Scots fir protected by a drystone wall, had been planted on the shoulder of the Hog Hill when the farm had belonged to the Earl of Wemyss. At least half a dozen pairs of herons nested on the highest trees, which had few branches. In spite of difficulties we managed to reach some of the great round platforms on which the herons had built their nests. Looking up through the network of branches and twigs, we could see the sky-blue eggs but were unable to reach them round the wide rim of the nests. Instead we made a hole up through the interwoven branches directly under the eggs.

After the young were hatched we were curious to see what happened at feeding time when they made a great deal of noise. The mystery of regurgitation became quite clear, and we were surprised to see eels of all sizes being swallowed whole by the fledglings, and often several inches would be left protruding from their beaks long after the parents left.

On one occasion we took a fledgling home with the idea that it would become tame. Though we fed it well on small trout, it seemed to have a distinct preference for fingers. One day, when the sharp beak just missed an unprotected eye, we decided it was time to return him to the heronry.

In the middle of the First World War cutters with horses and jankers arrived and their cross-cut saws and axes laid the herons' wood low. The trees were hauled down to the foot of the hill, loaded onto the jankers and carried to the railway at Broughton. The herons sought new nesting trees, and for a year or two a few nested on the spruces in Polmood Wood. White Rig Wood at Hearthstane, which adjoined Hog Hill Wood, was the herons' natural choice and they soon occupied the tallest trees.

One pair chose quite a low tree which had a very unusual shape. It grew on a steep rocky face with a fairly straight bole about 12 feet in height. At some time the top had been damaged and all the growth had continued on a horizontal branch which grew out a good 8 feet before turning upwards in the normal way. The herons' nest was only halfway up the final stem and no great distance from the ground. The birds had evidently calculated that the bend and absence of foot holes would provide sufficient protection.

Some tall Scots firs at Blacklaw on Fruid were occupied for a few years by two or three nests. Eventually a small spruce wood nearing maturity at Kingledores close to Hopehead became the only heronry in the district. Here the herons' diet was not always confined to fish. Young mallard ducklings and water voles were among the items they selected for food. When the trees were eventually felled, the herons left the district.

I have described elsewhere how I was shown a well-camouflaged woodcock's nest with a sitting hen while on a school excursion to Gala Burn Wood. Breeding woodcock must have been quite common, for I soon knew nests that I had found without assistance.

Woodcock are very interesting birds but are little known to most people as they are elusive and tend to nest in unusual places. They are very early breeders. I once saw a nest with eggs on March 9th, and by the 15th there were more eggs but, alas, all had been cracked by hard frost. On another occasion I found a nest on April 7th with eggs near hatching on the unlikely site of the lower slopes of the Garelet facing the loch.

Few people have seen the woodcock's habit of carrying its young, and it is often thought that such a feat could not be possible. Any doubts I may have had were dispelled when one day I was walking through a sparse wood of fairly old trees with a very tall companion. We were facing a strongish wind when a woodcock rose some distance in front of us. It hung in the air battling against the wind and holding on to its chick suspended between its thighs. As it yielded to the force of the wind, it flapped its wings hard and came back, just missing my friend's face but giving him an unforgettable close-up view of mother and chick. Finding the load too heavy, the mother dropped to the ground some forty yards or so behind and we left her undisturbed. This airborne load must have been a heavy burden to the hen but an adult bird has very powerful thighs which have the dual purpose of assisting take-off as well as clamping round the body of a chick needing to be carried.

I was privileged to encounter such a spectacle on many subsequent occasions. One of these was a spring morning when I was on my way to attend to sheep and lambs. I was surprised to raise a brood consisting of two flying young and the mother carrying an almost full-grown chick. They flew slightly downhill, crossed a wall and dropped out of sight. When I passed that way a few minutes later, the same group took off again with the same passenger towards some wet waste ground lower down. Fairly late in the day when I came along the same route in the opposite direction, the group took wing, curled back overhead and landed again in the sanctuary of the marshy waste.

Perhaps it is the weakly member of the brood that is the one chosen for special care. I cannot be absolutely certain that it was the same individual that was carried by its mother each time on the occasion just described. It seemed to be the most likely conclusion and, if so, it was presumably the one that was weaker and less able to fly than the others in the brood. Over a number of years fairly frequent examples of chick carrying were seen above a marshy wood on the farm. The flights, all downhill and over a hazardous fence, seemed to show a local inherited tendency to carry their young.

Woodcock often bred successfully on Fruid, far from trees and the kind of habitat usually associated with this bird. Late broods were still weak in flight in the shooting season, and several instances of carrying occurred. They always involved downhill flight and caused much surprise even to experienced sportsmen who sometimes failed to identify the strange helicopter-like flying object.

A most spectacular instance occurred on Fruid when a line of guns was walking along a steep hill face. As the line approached a gully, a single woodcock carrying a well-grown chick rose opposite the top gun. A 'no shooting' instruction was called. The bird was evidently in trouble with its load and turned downhill, passing close over the heads of the sportsmen, none of whom had ever witnessed the phenomenon before.

Over the years I came across several instances of birds exhibiting great feats of bravery in order to protect their mates and their young. One of these occurred on the way to Broughton. When the era of motorised schoolchildren arrived, pupils from the higher reaches of Holmswater were driven to school at Broughton or to join a bus to take them on to Peebles High School. For perhaps a mile the road ran beside a stretch of moorland and the driver as well as the passengers began to notice the presence near the road of a very vocal grouse. In the morning he would wait for the approaching taxi on a raised tuft of heather. As it passed he took wing and escorted the vehicle for about a quarter of a mile, flying all the time at a level which gave him a view of the occupants and they of him. When the taxi returned at night, he sometimes repeated the performance. It was evident he was doing sentry duty for his nesting mate and only stopped his patrol in late autumn.

Some years later I witnessed another incident when driving back from Moffat on the road between the Beef Tub and the AA box. I was almost at the monument to the two coach drivers lost in snow when I noticed a grouse with her brood of tiny young scattered across the road. I stopped well back as she continued her attempt to keep her little ones moving. If they had been a day or two older she would have had no trouble but these were very young and small.

A car approached from the opposite direction and would have crushed most of the chicks had I not managed to stop it in time. The mother, who had been rushing about, ignored my presence and threw herself flapping and scratching at the front of the offending car before flying into the heather. The young were now in cover off the road and the car drove off at speed, apparently annoyed at being held up for such a trivial reason. Though I waited for some time, the mother remained out of sight and I often wondered if she might have injured herself in her attack on the car.

Our Borderland ceased to provide habitat for eagles around the middle of the nineteenth century. The last breeding pairs had inhabited the wild crags of Gameshope and Moffat Water. Peregrine falcons, however, have continued to live in this area without interruption and have increased in number. A nesting site on the Garelet was used continuously during my boyhood though not always successfully.

This safe site could be viewed without disturbance from the top of the gully known as the Hawk Linn. Unfortunately some nature photographers, with more enthusiasm than knowledge of their subject, attempted to set up an observation hide without considering the birds themselves. The falcons were forced to abandon their nest for another on the other side of the valley in a much more vulnerable position.

Although I was frequently able to watch peregrines on and around their nests, my most dramatic viewing occurred in a remote steep-sided valley near Loch Skeen. I was looking through field glasses at the rocks on the opposite face of the ravine and saw feathers on the rocky ledges. When I failed to find the expected fox lair, I turned the glasses on the rocky slope leading toward the White Comb and was surprised to see a most unusual shape against the sky. I kept the glasses trained on this object and, as the size and definition increased, I could recognise a peregrine carrying a pigeon in his talons. The bird landed on a ledge on the cliff face and emitted a shrill chatter to its mate. Immediately the hen bird swept from its nest, which I had failed to see, and seized the prey. She then ripped off the pigeon's feathers and skin before satisfying her ravenous hunger.

On another occasion on a cold early spring day when squally showers of hail and snow driven by a strong nor' easter alternated with short periods of bright sunshine, I had tried without success to catch up with a very elusive fox on the rocky slopes of the Garelet. As I was returning across the face on a path which passed above the Hawk Linn, I decided to look over at the nesting place of a peregrine which I had seen on the wing earlier in the day. Facing into the piercing wind which whistled up the gully with driving flakes of powdery snow, I peered over the edge. There, a few feet below, the peregrine sat swaying on a rowan bush, rising and falling with her wings half opening and closing with each movement of the branch. It took a few seconds for her to become aware of my intrusion. She then dropped like a stone straight down into the wind and flurrying snow.

On one occasion when I was walking on the Tweed hills I saw a peregrine chasing a flock of starlings. In close-packed formation they turned at great speed, dived and twisted this way and that to elude their faster pursuer, changing shape at every turn without a single straggler. The noise from the hundreds of wings whistling and hissing varied with every manoeuvre and was astonishing to see. The chase ended abruptly when the peregrine suddenly veered off and allowed the starlings to streak away low in the opposite direction.

Another predator has recently arrived, attracted by the vast tracts of woodland. The large and powerful goshawk is a deadly killer, and its introduction to the wildlife scene can only be viewed with some doubt or even misgiving and could have unwelcome results.

The introduction of the goshawk brings back memories of the attempt of the late F.R.S. Balfour in the 1920s to introduce capercailzies at Dawyck. These birds were, I believe, of Norwegian stock and settled quite happily among the larch plantations. Unfortunately they had a tendency to wander and in some quarters were treated as vermin. The young, like black game, remained clumsy and slow until late in the season, which made them easy prey for foxes.

An attempt some years ago to reintroduce ptarmigan in the Broadlaw area had mixed results. Most soon disappeared but one pair took up residence around the Broadlaw heights with the craig as their safety retreat. The situation of their habitat could have assured their survival but unfortunately the pair were shot by a party who had leased the shooting from the Forestry Commission, who then owned the land.

Stories about the coming of the 'hawk owls' in the 'moosy' years of the 1890s aroused my youthful interest in short-eared owls. When a shepherd told me of a nest on Hazelbush Hill near the head of Tweed, I went off to find it. It was like searching for the proverbial needle in a haystack to find the nest in the wide, benty (rough grass) hillside. Although I never found the nest, I did locate three of the young, all of different ages in different places. As they were not yet able to fly, they were quite easy to catch and I took one which still had some down round his ears and neck. His defence was mainly his snapping beak and long, sharp claws which could penetrate deeply enough to draw blood.

When I got him home I was only allowed to keep him after I had promised to look after him myself. He was installed in a spacious cage

Andrew Lorimer with his pet owl.

made from a wooden box with a bar to sit on and a wire mesh door in front. As it was midsummer, there were plenty of voles available for they abounded under hay ricks that were then being moved for winter storage in sheds or stacks. Jackie, as we called him, could swallow a full-sized vole even though he was quite young and needed at least one per day. As the year progressed, mice became more difficult to find, and sometimes he had to make do with rabbit and small birds.

Jackie's feeding habits were a source of intense interest and some youthful wonder. He swallowed whole mice, voles and small birds head first and sometimes would run up and down the carcase before-hand, evidently breaking the larger bones and skull with his beak.

After eating he would sit back on his perch perfectly motionless for hours. All the time, however, the internal process of separating the flesh of his victim from the bones, fur and feathers went on and the unwanted materials were wound into a compact ball and regurgitated. He could regurgitate the 'pellet' successfully as long as he got enough feathers or fur in which to wrap the bones. At times it was difficult to find food. Once, in desperation, he was given small trout which he treated like mice. The pellet, containing the bones, was regurgitated without difficulty, with the small bones lying in the same pattern and direction as the fur and feathers of his usual diet.

There was plenty of room in the byre and his cage was fixed on a wall where he could see everyone coming and going. Whenever possible he was given the freedom of the byre, and though he sometimes flew outside he soon returned indoors. Members of the household whom he knew well were tolerated in an aloof manner but strangers were treated as enemies and his feathers would rise and, with outstretched wings, he hissed his dislike in no uncertain manner. My grandmother was with us then and she would visit him at least once a day and talk to him. Apart from myself, she was the only person he would treat without suspicion.

Early one spring when Jackie was about two years old, one of our cows developed milk fever and was unable to get to her feet unaided. Archie Anderson (Jim's father) came to help us. It was dark and the only light was from a swinging paraffin lamp. The strange voice and unusual activity upset Jackie, who happened to be in the rafters, and he flew out of the open door. It was a wild and windy night and it seemed that Jackie was lost.

At this time I cycled daily to Broughton to catch the train to Peebles High School. One of the pupils on the train, who came from Wrae dairy farm some five miles down the valley, mentioned that the previous night an owl had flown into the byre when they were milking and had roosted on the rafters. I had to see if it was Jackie and it was. He seemed very glad to see me and we went home together on my bicycle. He perched with his claws dug deeply into the raincoat which was wrapped round the handlebars. He appeared to enjoy the journey and occasionally looked round to be reassured of my presence.

Once home, Jackie was given even more freedom but the same situation involving a cow arose the following year. Once again he escaped into the darkness but this time the weather was much worse and we never saw him again.

The habits of our smallest birds and their ability to survive in adverse conditions have always been of great interest to me. Among these is the treecreeper, which is one of the smallest and least known. At

Mossfennan we became acquainted at close quarters. A large Wellingtonia Pine grew quite close to the house and the thick layer of soft bark provided an ideal place for their unique roosting holes. These smooth cups accommodated the little creatures so perfectly that, when occupied, the bark and their back feathers blended perfectly and the pattern of the tree trunk was unbroken. Only a small white drip denoted their overnight occupation.

Starting at about eye level, the little eggcup-sized holes could be seen well up the tree, mainly on the sheltered side. When looking at the colony by flashlight, it was evident that each bird had fluffed its feathers to exclude draughts and increase warmth. The highest number of holes I counted was eleven, and some were occupied all the year round.

One winter disaster struck. There was a large turnip pit in the stackyard where a heap of turnips was built up and covered by dry bracken to keep out the frost. At one end was a section filled with potatoes. These were being attacked by mice, so when a part-white stoat started to frequent the pit he was left to deal with the rodents. This he did quite well until one snowy morning his tracks appeared all round the great tree. I realised that he was climbing the trunk to reach the sleeping birds. Later, when some bailed hay in the corner of an open shed was used, the stoat's winter nest was exposed. He had made it warm and comfortable, and it consisted entirely of treecreeper feathers. So many had been killed that only the higher holes continued to be occupied.

Our variable climate occasionally produces extreme conditions at unusual times of the year. In the spring of 1963 storms and low temperatures came after some of the migrant birds had arrived. In one day, without paying undue notice, I saw two cuckoos and a redstart which had succumbed to the cold. In the severe winter and spring of 1978/79 the conditions in this area affected most non-migratory birds. Wrens, our smallest native bird, were much reduced in number. Their communal roosting habit did not, in this instance, save them, and in the summer of 1979 few were to be seen.

Heather wrens were once thought by some to belong to a different breed. As the name implies, they are to be found feeding among the longer heather near the hill burns and beyond the furthest territory of their larger cousin the dipper. The Scots name 'Heather Wran' is now hardly known. When the miners and others fished the Tweed during the Glasgow Fair holidays, they sometimes used a little brown fly with upright wings with their horsehair casts which they called the 'Wran's

Tail'. I do not know whether this name came from the source of the feathers or from the shape of the fly.

In the summer of 1980 I was agreeably surprised to find two different broods of wrens, and it is to be hoped their numbers will soon rise. Later, in one of the most remote haunts, I had the company of the Heather Wran busy, and even noisy, as though he or she had a mate within earshot.

An instance of quick progress in the education of young wrens occurred in my garden. When the fledglings left the nest, their parents were extremely busy finding and carrying them food. Almost the next day when one of the old birds was turning over some leaves under a holly bush, she apparently found some suitable insect life. She summoned one of her offspring with the usual 'trr-trr', and as soon as it lit beside her she left it to fend for itself and made off to repeat the operation with another member of her family.

Everyone who walks beside our rivers and burns is familiar with the rounded form of the dipper. His dumpy appearance and bobbing habit remind one of his smaller cousin the wren. At first glance this bird looks black, but on closer examination the plumage will be seen to be a very rich shade of dark brown. A white sash, more conspicuous in the cock bird, does not extend all round the body.

The dipper is an early nester and often chooses a site overhanging the water. Waterfalls and even positions lashed with spray are favoured. Their nests, like those of the wren, are constructed from moss which is gathered wet and firmly woven into its surroundings with an opening low on the side. The eggs, laid in early April, are white, slightly pointed and are usually four or five in number. When the hen bird is sitting, her mate can be seen on constant guard nearby.

Although he is an underwater feeder, the dipper does not have webbed feet but walks along the gravelly bottom of the burns looking for the insect larvae and aquatic life that forms his diet. Fish eggs and even small minnows are devoured and he can be seen operating behind the salmon redds (spawn), evidently picking up stray ova. On one occasion I saw a dipper attacked by a large cock salmon. The bird was only a foot or two from the edge of a gravel bed when the fish came across the stream with such speed that it ran itself up and onto the bank. The bird was so nearly caught that it surfaced on the salmon's back. Its strong short wings, which could be employed like fins to keep his body down and then to bring him quickly to the surface, had enabled him to escape.

The dipper's song differs from his small cousins' 'hurring' sound and includes several clear, fairly loud warbled notes. Large stones are selected for his performance, preferably situated where there is resonance from surrounding rocks or surfaces to augment the volume. A dipper could be seen and heard almost daily on a stone in the Logan Burn where the old Talla railway and the present Tweed road run close together. Even severe weather did not deter him, and the added echo from the arch of the road bridge doubled the effect of his song. The rocks at Carlow's Bridge provided another singing place in sight of a pleasant nesting site at the top waterfall.

When ice forms on the river, the dipper can be seen dropping down over the edge to carry on his submarine activities below the ice. When the main streams are completely covered, he retreats up the tributaries nearer the ice-free springs where the unfrozen waters afford him access to his underwater food. He is indeed a determined and successful survivor.

When looking for birds or their nests, there was always the likelihood that some completely different and unexpected creature might be seen. One such occasion came when, as a young schoolboy, I and some friends were searching the Menzion moss, a wide stretch of level moor at the foot of Quarter Hill between the Talla and Menzion roads. This was where several pairs of peewits and sometimes a pair of curlews would nest. On this particular day I caught a glimpse of a green lizard diving into a tuft of grass. One day we managed to capture one of these elusive creatures only to be horrified to be left with the tail while the rest of the body disappeared quickly into the thick vegetation. This was, of course, the normal way for lizards to escape in times of emergency. These lizards were usually about five inches long, most of which was tail, and their colours blended into the greenish surroundings.

One summer the roadmaking stone, which was stacked near the school, had not been entirely used and we became aware that the remaining section had been chosen as a safe haven for a family of tiny lizards only about two inches long. They looked very different to the ones we had seen in the Menzion moss. These were various shades of grey which matched exactly the stone in which they rested. They were never visible in dull or rainy weather but if the sun shone and warmed the grey whinstone, they could be seen sunning themselves, still and motionless. Although they appeared to be asleep, they were in fact entirely alert, and it only took a careless movement or a passing shadow to send them scurrying back into the dark recesses of the stone.

The shyness and elusiveness of these creatures could be circumvented if one was very careful. If one moved slowly and kept one's shadow well out of the way, it was possible to approach near enough to make a capture. One captive found its way into school one afternoon safely enconced in a warm pocket, but someone 'clyped' (gave the game away) and the schoolmaster sent the pupil out to liberate the lizard. It was released on the gravel at the edge of the playground where it was quite at home and was seen several times among the stones. When the summer holidays ended, the stone heap had gone and, although the young lizards had grown, their survival was doubtful. The species will still be around but that particular habitat is now a car park.

My interest in otters began with the incident I have described elsewhere when I saw my first otter one cold, icy morning on my way to school. This started me on the trail of one of the most interesting and least understood denizens of our Tweedsmuir waters. The once spectacular waterfalls at Tweedsmuir have changed since I first knew them, proving that the rocks and the hills are not so everlasting after all. The rocks at one side of the lower fall were impossible to scale in the upstream direction, and on the other side only one cleft allowed upward passage. The fall itself poured outwards enough to make ascending fish show themselves in leaps plainly visible to onlookers from the bridge. The way, however, was impassable for the otters who had to leave the water and follow the cleft upwards. In snow the tracks were clearly visible and it surprised me to find they were passing nightly.

Even in summer and autumn otter traffic passed downward by effortless water chute and upwards by the groove in the rock, leaving some loose grass or even sand in the narrow passage. I was now anxious to find out where they lived. On fishing expeditions I found a holt a mile or so above Tweedsmuir and I once disturbed another behind a slab of rock in the waterfalls of Fruid. But I found that their main abode was in the wilderness of Fruid Lakes. I was now able to notice the evidence of their presence in half-eaten fish, spraint at special places and runs where they had used their tobogganing form of downhill travel. At night-time, when fishing, I quite often encountered otters without actually seeing them.

Many years later one late September, I drove up to Fruid Lakes (before the dam had been built) with some food for a brood or two of wild pheasants which had hatched and survived in the surrounding hills. Small potatoes, fallen apples, vegetable peelings with some light oats and weed seeds from the threshing were scattered in the right places. These were soon found and augmented the feathered marsh dwellers' usual diet of seeds and crowfoot bulbs.

The stream in the centre of these bog lands had at one time been controlled by earthen banks. These were now broken in several places and the spreading water had made deep incursions into the surrounding ground, making it difficult and possibly dangerous to pass through in flood time. To make matters worse the coarse marsh grass had grown shoulder high in places on the raised banks and made it impossible to be sure of the next foothold. On this occasion I was following the stream where it ran between raised banks with both sides covered in long reed grass, when I became aware of a strange piping sound which I had never heard before. It was so haunting and plaintive that it has remained in my memory ever since.

At first I thought it was some bird but everywhere was deserted and the sound, like the note of a flute, seemed to come from ground level. My spaniel was equally interested and, as we stood stock still listening, her ears were pricked and she pointed her head across the burn. The strange notes rose and fell and even stopped at times. Without speaking, I signalled my dog to go, she disappeared into the undergrowth and the sounds stopped. After some little time she reappeared on the opposite bank and stood looking alternatively at me and over her shoulder.

I then went upstream where I could cross and join her on the other side and followed her into the thick reeds. She soon stopped and pointed at what, at first, seemed a rumpled clump of vegetation. She then shot her head into an opening in the heap and dropped at my feet a young and very unhappy otter pup about the size of a half-grown rabbit. It was fat with thick brown fur and a cream underside.

The nest, well up above flood level, contained three young otters. It was roofed with pulled-up reeds, and below was an inner structure of short dry grass. It was a larger version of the nest a hedgehog might make. There were two openings to the nest, which was warm and perfectly dry. The thatch for the roof had come from reeds nearby and some force must have been used as they are not easily pulled up. It was perfect thatching with bundles of reeds placed all round the structure so that the bends were in the middle and the ends were lying sloped outwards and downwards. The material was still fresh and green and, while the inside may have been older, the roof was quite recent. When I returned the pup to its nest, it crept in beside its mates. This unexpected encounter had made my day. It had been a wonderful experience which I was never to forget.

By the 1950s the otter population was quite numerous. Some were being seen and even killed or injured on the roads. At various times my spaniels brought me very young specimens but were always gentle with them. Then came a time which boded ill for all the dwellers in Fruid Lakes. One of the adjoining farms was sold to the Forestry Commission, and the Lakes were part of the land to be flooded to form a new reservoir to supply the needs of Edinburgh. The otters remained until the end when the great machines, the noisy monsters, started to construct the dam itself. The world of our otters, the snipe, the woodcock, the duck, the kestrels and migrating deer was soon to become only a memory to a very few.

During my lifetime many forms of wildlife seem to be losing the struggle for survival while others seem to flourish. The orange tip butterfly has only recently formed colonies in the more southern parts of the Borders, and some warm spells have provided good breeding conditions for birds like swallows. Some summer visitors, however, now seem scarce, especially the cuckoo and redstart. Even flycatchers, the tiny warblers once so very common, are no longer plentiful.

Birds like sand martins, sandpipers, song thrushes, moorhens and sparrows are all now under-represented in this area. One winter visitor, the snow bunting, has been an absentee for several seasons. It was an unforgettable sight to see the elongated flock drifting along the snow wreaths (drifts), with pure white specimens showing up here and there. On moorland curlews and golden plovers are thinner on the ground, and the peewit has all but disappeared. The resurgence of the peregrine falcon a few years ago seems to have subsided possibly through dearth of food.

The large-scale planting of coniferous trees in the Upper Tweed valley has not only altered the landscape but has also made it a less attractive habitat for a large number of birds and animals. I can only give thanks that I was able to explore the area and become acquainted with its wildlife before these changes began.

Chapter Ten *Gun Dogs*

My association with gun dogs did not begin very auspiciously. I was still at the Tweedsmuir school and in the shooting season acted as beater and game carrier for shoots over Hearthstane, Menzion and Fruid. The shooting party did not have dogs of their own and each year hired what were supposed to be working dogs. Before long I was always given one of these to work. One spaniel, which I had for two seasons, gave me endless trouble. He was almost uncontrollable and had to be kept on a lead most of the time. He was more trouble than he was worth.

One year things improved and I had a fairly old female labrador with completely opposite characteristics. She belonged to a gamekeeper and so was very obedient and would only move under orders. But she had lost the joy of living and would not work more than a short distance away. I decided if I ever had a gun dog of my own I would train it without the defects of these two.

That opportunity arrived in an unexpected way and involves the story of Jock, a most remarkable animal. I must start the story at the beginning when the most famous breed of spaniels at that time was the Avondales bred by the Duchess of Hamilton. She relied on the keepers on the Douglas Estate for training, which they did to full field trial standard demanded by the Kennel Club.

One very good dog, Champion X of Avondale, was mated secretly with a local bitch of the old Scottish type – black and tan. The resulting litter were quickly disposed of except for the runt, a small darkish black and tan. A local farmer took him in for his wife's sister who lived near the town with a large house and grounds. A few months later the pup contracted a skin disease and was brought back to the farm. Here one of the servant girls made a coat to take the place of the hair he lost and my brother, who was a shepherd there, took him to the hill along with his collies. New hair grew, the coat was removed and in due course he was returned to his suburban home, sleek and healthy.

The farmer moved to Peeblesshire and my brother, now married, moved there too. The dog, called Jock, had meantime become reinfected with eczema and had once again come under my brother's care. His

151

wife was equally involved in Jock's welfare and eventually his recovery was complete. He was now two years old and should by now have been trained but an unfortunate experience had interfered with his interest in living creatures. Outside my brother's cottage a hen tended a brood of chicks and Jock, following his instincts, had grabbed one, killing it instantly. My brother, who was nearby, gave him a hard cuff with his hat and Jock disappeared into the cottage with his tail between his legs and hid beneath a bed. There he remained for the rest of the day until he eventually emerged still looking unhappy. After that incident, although he would accompany my brother, he would never retrieve game for him.

At this time I was attending Moray House, the teacher training college in Edinburgh. One afternoon when returning to Tweedsmuir from college I found all the roads blocked with fallen trees and so stayed the night with my brother and his wife. Jock treated me as a friend, and when the roads were still blocked the next day I took him with me to help the rabbit catcher. With difficulty I got Jock to retrieve a few rabbits. He gradually became familiar with gunshots and a few commands, and last thing at night I would give him a short lesson with cold stiff rabbits. Unfortunately I had only short spells with him for quite a while.

When his owner heard that Jock had a desire to work, he arranged for him to continue his career with me. At this point my brother took my father's place at Hearthstane in Tweedsmuir. I was now helping at most shoots in the district, so Jock had plenty of work and exercise. He worked perfectly on furred game but still would not lift feathered creatures although he would find them without difficulty.

One day I shot a partridge which fell into a watery ditch. Surprisingly, Jock arrived with the soaking corpse which he had picked up without noticing the feathers. I got him to bring it over after it had dried out and gave him much praise and encouragement. The next morning I took off to the hill and sent him for a newly shot grouse. He picked it up but immediately dropped it. Sensing that he was meant to bring it, he eventually picked it up and hesitatingly delivered it to me.

The final accomplishment, to retrieve from across water, came easily to Jock. We started by swimming side by side from bank to bank of the river, and very quickly he learned to retrieve by swimming across on his own.

What glorious days were to follow, especially one never-to-be-forgotten college holiday. At the first hour of daylight Jock and I would set out on my motorbike, with Jock sitting before me on the petrol tank, never moving until we reached our destination. This was some five miles away where I had to inspect lines of snares and, with Jock's help, find any rabbits that had escaped still attached to a snare. When we returned home I had to gut the rabbits, couple them and get them to Broughton station where they were put into hampers, weighed and labelled and sent off to be in the city market by 10am.

Our next task was to attend to the young pheasants and their foster mothers. They were fed, watered and their coops moved onto fresh ground. Care had to be taken to make sure that there was shade at all times of the day and that all precautions had been taken to protect the birds from vermin, crows and buzzards. After this it was back to the snares. These had to be kept in good repair, replaced as necessary and set ready for the night. After tea Jock and I would set off for the river where he would sit patiently while I fished.

Jock found fishing very dull. He disliked the swish of the line through the air, hated the cold sliminess of the catch and was bored to death by what seemed to him the many unnecessary commands. Yet, in spite of this aversion, he once rose nobly to the occasion when I found myself in a tight spot. My rod had broken and left me with a 12lb salmon splashing beside the gravel. Jock plunged in and held the struggling fish until I was able to grasp its gills and pull it safely to the shingle.

So began the working life of one of the best dogs in the country and a partnership in which I was honoured to share. We attended shoots far and wide on my motorbike. For some reason Jock had a strong distrust or fear of a camera and never looked comfortable unless he was completely unaware that he was being photographed. At work, however, he was in his element and in his devotion to duty never lost a bird or animal, whether it was grouse, partridge, snipe, black game, woodcock, wild duck or hares, nor left one maimed to die.

An important guest on one shoot wished to buy a highly qualified field trial dog and arranged for two winners to demonstrate their prowess on grouse. At his butt he had seven birds to collect but after the ground had been thoroughly covered in great style by the two candidates, only three birds had been found. Most of the party and beaters were watching and nothing more seemed to be happening until someone called 'send Curly's spaniel down'. I sent Jock back to come in against the wind and he approached between the quartering pair and brought a bird from between their noses. This was repeated until

Andrew Lorimer with two of his spaniels.

only one bird was missing. The frustrated gun insisted it must still be there and asked me to recall Jock when he wanted to go too far away.

The search was called off, and as I was taking the beaters to the next drive, one of the keepers called to me to whistle in my dog. Jock had found the missing grouse and was running from person to person looking for his master. He became much admired for such incidents of great ability and many others showing great courage and ingenuity. The excellence of his work was only equalled by his complete trust in and devotion to me. He ended his days in honourable retirement in a household consisting of his other great love – children.

My next dog, a bitch, came to me in somewhat unusual circumstances. Near Soonhope in Peebles, where my father had retired, were several small wooden houses which today would be called chalets. They were primitive and small and most were occupied only in summer. One, however, was occupied all the year by a retired gamekeeper who had spent most of his life on a neighbouring estate and chose to live here in his retirement with his dogs as company. The dogs were spaniels of a strain that he had bred and worked all his life. At this time his stock was down to two from the same litter. One was a bold, strong-natured dog and the other a smaller and shyer black and white bitch. The dog had to be handled with a firmness which so disturbed the gentler sister that she lost confidence to retrieve and showed signs of becoming gun-shy.

Binnie, as the old keeper was called, approached my father and explained the situation and asked if I would take on the rehabilitation of the young bitch. At this time I was an assistant teacher and came home only at weekends. At the next opportunity I visited Binnie and agreed to take the bitch and arranged I would breed from her and he would get a bitch from the litter.

Nell, as she was called, had a lovely gentle nature and I did not start her working for quite a while. Meanwhile, as part of her training she was being taught to remain where told to stay. When I was ploughing fields by tractor, she lay on a coat or jacket knowing I would appear at the end of each furrow.

One day I was cutting grass among trees near Mossfennan and laid my jacket down for her to lie on. The farm cat at this time had a small quarter-grown kitten which had become very friendly with Nell and lived in an open shed at the back of the house. All went well while Nell could see me but when I passed behind a large tree she disappeared. When I came in sight again I noticed she had gone. I should have gone after her immediately but I wanted to finish the mowing. When I next came in sight she had returned, and when I had finished and came back for my jacket she looked at me apologetically as though asking to be forgiven. There, between her paws, was the happy kitten playing with the ends of her big glossy ears. She had fetched her little friend to keep her company.

Nell became a very good dog, obedient, bold and wise and, I should add, beautiful. I was now married and lived in East Lothian but spent most weekends at Mossfennan. My car stayed there as I had a grant of petrol coupons from the Department of Agriculture for fox control. My journey back to Tweedsmuir was by bus and was made in three laps. The first was to North Berwick, the second to Edinburgh and the third to Broughton. My wife always made the journey late on Friday afternoon with Nell and left me to find my way after school.

On one occasion the bus from North Berwick was crowded and my wife got the last seat. Nell slipped under the seat as usual but about four miles on at Dirleton, when my wife helped the passenger in the adjoining seat to get off the bus, Nell got off too. My wife reboarded the bus and only noticed Nell's absence when halfway to Edinburgh. She left the bus, took another back and found Nell at the Dirleton stop looking very worried, patiently waiting for the return of her mistress. Her early training in the plough-field had been justified.

Nell was mated and produced a litter with only one female pup which, of course, went to Binnie. The mating was intended to be with a very good dog of Binnie's choice but a really big snowstorm came on and all roads became impassable. Fortunately there was a suitable mate quite near. At the aerodrome at East Fortune a married airman had been called away to start flying from a southern airfield. He eventually found accommodation for his wife but not for the dog, which was left with a retired couple only a mile or two away. This dog, a very well bred spaniel, saved a difficult situation and was mated with Nell. Binnie eventually bred with Nell's bitch and most of those pups went to keepers as working dogs.

After Nell died I did not need a dog until after the war, in 1947, by which time I had given up teaching and was farming at Mossfennan. Binnie sent me his choice from the last pair of a big litter. We called her Trixie, an unusual name for a most unusual spaniel. Her training, by tone of voice, hand signals and a few whistled commands from a distance, was a pleasure to me and equally so to her. If she had a fault it was for being a one-man dog. Her versatility was most surprising and came from her innate ability to understand a situation. She even helped when working with sheep and could find lost lambs alive or dead in all weathers. She accomplished so many unusual feats in the course of her work that it is only possible to describe a few. One, which I have already mentioned elsewhere, was the time when she found the otter's nest in the bogs of Fruid.

Another example of Trixie's remarkable ability took place at home. The outbuildings at Mossfennan were scattered, and some young cattle were housed a short distance away in an old mill, part of which held hay bales and other fodder. Some bantams had the freedom of this building and had a habit of laying eggs overnight in the feeding troughs. When filling the troughs and racks with hay one morning, I picked up only one egg which I laid on a nearby bale and went on with the feeding. At this time Trixie had two pups two months old, and when I heard a slight growl I turned to see what was happening. The two pups were trying to jump onto the bale to get the egg and Trixie was telling them to stop. Sometime later when I was mixing food back in the main building, Trixie and her pups appeared. Something in her demeanour seemed strange. She came right up to my feet and laid down the bantam egg and stood guarding it from the eager pups with a look that upbraided me for my carelessness.

Hayfields had to be kept free of molehills, and when our fields flooded moles were confined to knolls just above flood level and could be found by a good dog just below the surface. During one flood we had been fairly successful when Trixie started pointing into the drystone walls. Here we found moles that had escaped the rising waters by climbing up the spaces between the stones. When we finished and were passing a group of Scots fir trees, Trixie stopped and pointed behind one of the trunks. I went round to see what interested her and was most surprised to find a mole six feet up the tree hanging on with his long sharp claws in one of the rough grooves characteristic of Scots firs. A rabbit trapper once told me of a similar instance involving a rabbit which he found still clinging to a fence although the flood had subsided.

At this time the main house at Mossfennan was run as a hotel, and one day a guest who was returning to his work in the Middle East oilfields wanted to spend one last day on the hills. Although it was rough weather, I took him out onto the hills beyond Tweedsmuir with a keeper. A small covey of partridges came back high overhead and one was killed. In the wind it fell quite a distance away among rough grass and rushes.

I was in a much higher position and able to look down on the ground in question, so when the keeper's dog failed to find the partridge, I sent down my young dog. He too failed to find it but at one point he followed a hill drain and splashed through a pool at its source. Now it was Trixie's turn, and almost straight away she reached the pool and stood pointing at the water. I called her off and gave her another cast but she still persisted in returning to point at the rushy pool. So I had to go down and see for myself.

I realised that Trixie thought the bird was somewhere under the surface so I took off my jacket, got down on my knees and started sweeping my hand and arm through the pool as far as I could. First I got only handfuls of decaying grass and then found the sodden object of our search. Neither the keeper nor the guest had seen anything like this before, but I knew the secret of Trixie's success. The partridge fell so fast that it carried well under the surface and my young dog, floundering in the pool, probably pushed it down further. But bubbles of scented air from under the feathers still rose to the surface and from these Trixie had made the right deduction.

I was still involved in fox control, covering probably 40,000 acres. Trixie could tell the presence of a fox at least 150 yards away above ground. In finding foxes underground she made only one mistake, and an understandable one, by marking an earth into which a fox had recently carried a newly killed grouse. She was still working well at eleven years old though her speed had diminished. When at last she had to be put down I called in a vet. In such circumstances it is hard to remain unemotional but I always remember her with the feeling that she felt great joy in accomplishing the slightest wishes of her master.

Trixie's progeny distinguished themselves as thoroughly reliable gun dogs, but for some time I kept only two of her sons. One, Dandy, was a very handsome animal, rather large, gentle and of excellent conformation and stamina. The other was the only dog in Trixie's last litter bred from a dog with some show blood. He had a very difficult nature but people who came to have bitches mated invariably chose him rather than Dandy. One breeder took him away for a whole breeding season as a stud dog. Eventually Dandy was mated with a very good dog from Dumfriesshire. I could have had a male from him but I didn't need a dog at the time and let him go.

In spite of his size Dandy was very athletic, but his outstanding characteristic was the gentle way he handled live game and other creatrures. He could carry lambs, kittens, cats and young otters with such care that they didn't even struggle.

I bred a litter from a bitch of the best field trial performers in the country, but of the three females only one bred and she died young – probably poisoned. So I still did not have a breeder. Some of my breed from Dandy survived on an estate in Ayrshire but by this time I had been given a young labrador and didn't follow them up.

Dogs have played a very significant part in my life, and each has been a great companion. Devotion to duty is looked upon as a virtue by us humans. In dogs it is a character trait which is only cultivated from outside by careful training, or given freely from within as an expression of great love. We can never know how much the words of praise, 'good dog', mean to our so-called dumb friends and we can never quite measure how much they are willing to do to earn them.

Chapter Eleven *Keeping the Past Alive*

The changes that have taken place during the last half of the twentieth century could never have been envisaged in the early 1900s. Means of travel, for example, have changed so dramatically that a generation has grown up never knowing the roadside landmarks once familiar to everyone.

Milestones are seldom seen now, and the measurements recorded when these red sandstone pillars were erected have been made incorrect by road realignment. A few still hold their heads above ground but most have disappeared. In their heyday they were about a foot wide and three or four feet high. They were sited on either side of the road, and each was exactly 1760 yards (one mile) from its neighbour. With their rounded tops and convenient height they provided a handy seat for the weary wayfarer. In addition to the surveyor's mark they showed the exact mileage to the centre of Edinburgh, taken to be the GPO at the junction of Princes Street and the North Bridge.

Horse troughs were situated only where water was available and were fed by a pipe or open spout from a waterway or spring. Most were of cut freestone and measured two or three feet long by about two feet wide and were little more than one foot deep. They were looked after by the roadmen who made sure that this all-important refreshment was available to beast and man if required.

Two troughs, one on Stanhope Brae and one between Rowan Bank and Forest Hill, were especially interesting to me as they were tenanted by freshwater newts. These tiny, harmless amphibian creatures with beautifully streamlined bodies are a perfect example of nature's handiwork.

A unique landmark that has survived is a cairn close to the junction of the Menzion and Talla roads. It is made out of an ancient quern crowned by a tapering water-rounded stone pointing upwards. This acts as a signpost with the destination of the two roads marked in black and white on large smooth stones.

No sign, however, remains of the nearby curling pond which occupied a triangular hollow bounded by a strong turf wall parallel with the Menzion road and another along the Talla road. The pond could accommodate four rinks and was looked after by Adam Dempster, a

Curling pond, *c.* 1900.

versatile man, a skilled fencer, dyker, grave digger and drainer, who lived at Dykehead opposite the schoolhouse. The task of looking after the curling pond was a very important one which had also been performed by his ancestors.

The pond was controlled by an outlet drain which Adam Dempster closed in late autumn and opened in spring to let the water away. At such a height above sea level the pond froze for longer than any of those lower down the valley, and a great deal of curling took place. The Tweedsmuir Curling Club had existed for decades without a curling shed, but following a series of good curling winters, the need for some kind of shed became more pressing. In the famous winter of 1892 the pond remained frozen for eight weeks and allowed continuous play against rinks from all over the county and beyond. At an end-of-season dinner the question of a shed was raised once again and it was agreed that one should now be erected.

The local worthies, usually known by the names of their farms, donated the materials for the structure: one gave sheets of galvanised iron, another the wooden framework, others gave a stove and fuel. All the members took part in the work. The 'Curlin' Hoose' was erected a few yards from the Talla road and a similar distance from the bank at the corner of the L-shaped pond.

The result was a simple tin shed about 10′ by 15′ which was

anything but beautiful. The door and a window of four panes of glass, each about one foot square, occupied much of the side facing the pond. The floor was earthen except at one end where a small, round American-type stove stood on a large flagstone. The chimney consisted of a 4-inch iron drain pipe which protruded about a foot through the arched roof. This stove could be used for brewing tea or other beverages, for the 'Roaring Game' was known to be 'sair on the throat'.

Successive generations of schoolchildren hid behind the walls of the shed and used the blue-grey galvanised iron to try out their newly acquired skills of writing with lead pencils. Names, addresses, dates, drawings (mainly of horses' heads) and printed initials of supposed lovers all vied for places within reach of the wide range of scribblers. The sides hidden from open view were more thickly covered than the rest.

On one panel, in excellent writing, was a complete poem attributed to Mary Tweedie-Stodart, on the damming of Talla:

> Dwellers in Auld Reekie feeling rather dry
> Search the country over for a new supply
> So they come to Tweedsmuir to taste the waters there
> And find no other streamlets can with these compare.

The verses continued, telling the story of the building of the dam which trapped the waters of Talla and Gameshope for Edinburgh's thirsty citizens. The verses were set to the tune of 'Riding Down To Bangor' and its rhythm of a train may have been inspired by the local 'pug' chugging round Cockiland towards the dam with its half-dozen small trucks of puddle clay, used for the basis of the dam.

Another panel seemed almost empty, but on examination the reason appeared in a distinct statement in the middle written in large letters:

> FOOLS' NAMES ARE LIKE THEIR FACES
> TOO OFTEN SEEN IN PUBLIC PLACES.

The work of the budding philosopher had evidently some psychological effect on the would-be graffittists, but only on this one panel, as names aplenty filled the others.

The First World War reduced the enthusiasm for the 'Roaring Game'. The young men had gone, many never to return, and sombre shadows fell across the lives of many of those whose cheery voices had echoed over the ice. Only the curling shed remained, standing by itself under the bank of the pond. Some time during or just after the Second World

The Insh.

War the structure disappeared, and one wonders if the curling club, to whom it belonged, was then officially dissolved or just forgotten. The flattened sheets of the curling shed are completely hidden under layers of rotting vegetation at the bottom of the now almost unrecognisable curling pond.

Most of the budding writers, artists and poets have, like the 'Curlin' Hoose' itself, now gone from the Tweedsmuir scene. But some of those names inscribed on the panels can still be read on the war memorial at the entrance of the Kirk ... their names live on.

Means of transport before the First World War have become mere memories like the roadside landmarks that helped the travellers in those days. One method used in Tweedsmuir was unique and is worth recording. It concerned a small triangle of land called the Insh, which lies between Talla Water and the Tweed. Bounded by both rivers, the land was shared out between the Bield, which belonged to Oliver, Hearthstane, the Glebe and Menzion.

The small farm connected with the Bield had land on the Oliver side of the Tweed in addition to that in the Insh. When I was young, the Bield was farmed by Ritchie Ross, the local hirer of a wagonette and a brougham. He was then quite elderly and the farm work was largely carried out by his youngest daughter. As access to their land in the Insh by way of Carlowes bridge was time-consuming, old Ritchie and his daughter took the direct route by way of the river using stilts.

As can be imagined, the schoolchildren watched with admiration, especially at hay time, when both Ritchie and his daughter made the journey several times each day. Naturally we had to try to use these wooden leg extensions and made crude stilts of our own. Our greatest difficulty arose in finding suitable pieces of material. We then found it took some considerable time to master the technique and practised mainly on terra firma. Eventually some of us were able to add this adult accomplishment to our list of skills.

A family that I held in both awe and admiration was the Mastertons of the Green – one of the best-known families in Broughton. The Green, the local inn, was the largest house in the village but the name also applied to the farmland adjacent to the village. When Helen Masterton at the age of 18 married Buchan, the young Free Kirk Minister, the inn ceased to sell liquor in accordance with the teetotal tenets of the Church.

The three sons of the family, John, James and Ebenezer, all had strong personalities but different characters. Combined, they formed one of the most successful farming enterprises of the time. John Buchan considered that one of his uncles prayed, one swore and the third sang.

John, the eldest brother, was small and wiry and acted as bookkeeper and accountant. He was of a strongly religious turn of mind and, if at all possible, never missed attending the Broughton Free Kirk, of which he was an elder. For these occasions he wore his dickie and stiff white collar which came right up to his chin. He was something of a puritan in his attitude to drink and swearing and never allowed himself the use of strong language of any kind. I always felt that the spirit of evil was to him a very personal figure, something or someone almost visible.

One Sunday after Kirk John's two brothers fell into a very heated argument on a farming matter. Some strong language was used and John tried unsuccessfully to pacify the quarrelling pair. Tut-tutting and wringing his hands in despair, he exclaimed: 'Did ye ever hear the like and sic a day for the Deil'.

James was very different. He was of medium build, clean-shaven and in some ways resembled his illustrious nephew in the cast of his rather narrow features. As a boy he had acquired the pet form of his name and remained 'Jims' to his friends for the rest of his life. Much more forthright than John, his language when excited or upset was apt to become somewhat earthy and strong. When Buchan, in his wartime poem 'Home Thoughts', written in Scots, used the word 'mud', Jims's criticism was couched in no uncertain terms. 'They micht hae 'mud' in Oxford but it's 'glaur', plain 'glaur', oo've got at Bamflett'. That he should dare to express such an adverse opinion scandalised the rest of the household, though some were inclined to agree with him.

Eben, the youngest, was a more social character and much involved in the life not only of the locality but of the county as well. He often acted as chairman at concerts and similar events and had a repertoire of very Scottish songs which he delivered with a most expressive style of his own.

Though the three brothers carried on their farming enterprise as a partnership, the two older bachelor members lived at Bamfleet while Eben, who married Miss Tudhope of Broughton Place, occupied Burnetland. So successful were their farming efforts that by 1930 they owned not only The Green, Bamfleet and Burnetland but also The Cleugh, Gosland, The Crook, Fruid, Carterthope and Kilbucho Place.

My eldest sister Margaret (Peg) acted as housekeeper to the two brothers at Bamfleet for several years at the time I was travelling daily to Peebles High School from Tweedsmuir. During snowstorms when the roads were blocked I stayed there overnight and shared the regular household life, which was somewhat spartan and frugal. Porridge morning and night was the order of the day, every day. I had, until then, been used to having milk with porridge but now, because the cow was dry, the choice was a spoonful of either syrup or treacle.

One night when doing my homework, I was struggling with some of the grammatical perplexities of the Latin language when Jims leaned across the table and picked up one of my textbooks with the remark that he used to be 'quite guid at Layten'. After perusing a few pages, he pushed the book away and announced: 'A' think they be gane and changed it sin' a' was at the schule'.

When they bought cattle, the brothers often attended the northern markets and brought back large numbers of cattle by train. These were often highland animals with such great horns that they could not get through the standard doorways of the byres. The droves had to be taken from either Broughton or Biggar station and their arrival made quite a spectacle. I remember one evening after dark meeting a long train of these beasts, bedraggled and hungry, coming along the back road from Biggar. A dark figure was at the front and another brought up the rear, each swinging a paraffin lamp. The deep intermittent lowing of the shaggy animals and the bobbing lanterns gave an eery, almost frightening dimension to the procession.

In 1916 the Mastertons sold the Crook Inn at Tweedsmuir to the Camerons, whose Kingussie hotel had been taken over by the army. Eben called a day or so after their arrival and Willie Cameron was somewhat embarrassed because all that was to be found in the cellar was a bottle or two of chartreuse. He apologised for the lack of choice and explained that this was the drink of kings and emperors. Eben swallowed the liquid and, red in face and short of breath, spluttered, 'Kings and Emperors, did ye say?' and after a pause to regain his composure he continued, 'My God, Cameron nae wonder there's wars'.

While my recollections go back to the early years of the twentieth century, those of people I knew as a boy went back to the middle of the century before. The tale of the large fish run up Talla was recounted to me by two different people and that of the Garelet sheep in the great snow storm of 1890 was told by John Robertson, a life-long shepherd in Tweedsmuir. All these recollections and others I have described elsewhere have been passed on by word of mouth over the generations and have enabled the past to be kept alive.

An account of a basket night expedition was related to me by the late David Sharpe and referred to places in Scaur Water. As with many such recollections it concerned the shepherd's life and bad weather.

It wad be Mairch whan oo' gaed ower on a basket veesit to the Johnstons o' Glenherd. There were five o' us, my faither and mither, Jean (my sister), mysel and the young herd frae the neeboring hirsel across the burn. He was ca'd Airchie Carr and cam frae below the border. He was little mair than a callant [boy] an we whiles thocht his Cumberland tongue mair than a wee bit queer.

Tae get there we had tae cross twae rigs [ridges] an it took us a guid oor an a half. Maist o' the snow was away except for some drifts lying along the shooders on the dark side o' the rigs. The nicht passed ower quick wi a hand or twae o' catch the ten, a guid supper an' some sangs. The Johnstons were a' great singers. Geordie Johnston played the fiddle an we even had a bit dance on the kitched flair. The bottle o' whisky gaed roond an' everybody was cheery, especially Airchie.

At both sides o' the fire the Johnstons had easy chairs wi' casters on them. Airchie had never seen anything o' the kind in his life and was fair taken on wi the movin chairs. After the last dram for the road oo set off back ower the hill. The nicht was dry an' frosty and a'a gaed weel till oo reached the snow drifts.

This time we were comen in abune [above] the wreaths [snow drifts] an noo they were hard wi' the frost. In spite o' wairning Airchie, maybe a bit ower crouse [bold] wi' the whisky, decided tae cross ane o' the big drifts. After twae steps, doon he went on his backside an' away he gaed doon oot o' sicht ower the steep snow.

It was a wee while afore oo found him for oo had tae gang roon' aboot keepin' tae black grands. Ma sister got tae him first. 'Are ye hart Airchie?' 'I'm a' reat' cam the answer. Lookin' up at the wide sheet o' white she remarked: 'My Airchie ye slid a lang wey.' 'Ei,' he replied, 'an if I'd hed some o' them casters on me I could hev gyen te' Cerlisle'.

Throughout my early years at Hearthstane Andrew Anderson of Glenveg was a regular visitor. He was born in Megget in 1838 and went to Gameshope when he was three years old. As a shepherd he herded there and in Megget during the great storm and mousy years of the 1890s.

Later he farmed at The Cleuch at Kilbucho and Woodend near Wandel where he was our family's near neighbour. My elder brothers started shepherding with him, helping after school to drive the sheep to the higher ground. When he retired about 1900 Andrew and his brother William built Glenveg, a house standing by itself near the

Glenveg, with rowan arch at gate.

Picnic party at Gameshope. Miss Lang is second from left, with Andrew Anderson
in the back row.

Moffat road just over half-a-mile above the Crook Inn in Tweedsmuir.
When my family came to Hearthstane in 1910 we were once again
near neighbours.

When he laid out the ground around Glenveg Andrew was careful
to follow the old custom of planting rowan trees near the house.
Saplings planted on either side of the entrance eventually joined to
form a complete archway over the gate. It was believed that rowan
trees planted near a dwelling warded off evil and protected the inhabitants from the powers of the supernatural beings that were thought
to haunt the surrounding countryside.

Even now many traditional herds' cottages, some still occupied and
others mere ruins, have rowans nearby. Some of these trees are very
old and gnarled indicating that they were probably planted as a protection when the houses were built. In the outlying sheilings where
few other trees were to be seen, rowans were conspicuous, as for
example at Fingland, Badlieu, Tweedhopefoot, Tweedshaws, Gameshope, Over Menzion, kingledores Hopehead, and the Riggs. Some may
now be dead from age or cut down but they lived long enough to
afford the dwellers there a sense of security.

Andrew Anderson was a handsome, lively and sociable person, not very tall but straight. When I first knew him he was quite old, white haired and always walked with a stick. My father, among other activities such as stick making, also acted as unpaid barber to most of the neighbours including 'Auld Andra' who would joke about his diminishing crop. Andrew was a batchelor and after his sister died was looked after by a housekeeper, Janet Anderson (no relation) who was a particular friend of my sister Janet.

As Glenveg was quite capacious the main part of the house was let out in the summer months. One year the house was rented by Jean Lang who was a keen fisherwoman. It was she who encouraged my fishing by giving me the special Martin's Red Loop fly. She was particularly interested in recalling names and incidents from the past and in 'Auld Andra' she found a kindred spirit. One day she hired a carriage from Ritchie Ross and organised a trip to Gameshope. The party, which included Andrew, his housekeeper, my sister and Miss Lang, drove up Talla and had a picnic in surroundings familiar and dear to the old gentleman. The Talla Lakes by now had become the reservoir but Andrew's anecdotes of the past with the names of hills and glens added to the interest of the occasion.

He was very interested in wild life and in me he found an attentive and inquisitive listener. When relating incidents he used the old Scottish tongue and some words were included so naturally they must have been in general use by the previous generation. His sister Helen was spoken of as 'Eelen', the old form which resembled the gaelic.

He told me about the last of the eagles that nested in the Crags round Talla, with ravens sometimes as neighbours, of 'snowslips' (avalanches), floods on the lakes and runs of fish. He experienced the 'Moosie' years – that strange period in the 1890s when, in a few seasons, the vole population of the hills rose to a point where no grass was left for the sheep. Farmers who could pay for low ground grazing moved their stock, but those who could not lost their livelihood and became bankrupt.

The problem was eventually solved by nature herself. Great numbers of predators arrived in the area especially hawk owls, the short eared owls who hunted by daylight and at dusk. Andrew described how at nesting time they laid big clutches of eggs – up to a dozen or more – and how they hatched, not all at the same time but in succession with a day or two between each egg. In this way the earlier birds were fledged and away from the nest while the younger ones were keeping

Mr and Mrs Jimmy
Brown.

the remaining eggs warm. In the course of two summers the mice diminished and almost disappeared and the birds likewise.

Andrew Anderson died at Glenveg in August 1921 aged 83 and was buried in the Tweedsmuir churchyard.

James (Jimmy) Brown, a contemporary of Andrew Anderson, was born in 1847 in Manor Valley where his father was a shepherd. The family moved to Tweedsmuir when he was quite young and lived at Kingledores Hopehead. After he left school at Tweedsmuir he too became a shepherd and when he married Margaret Lindsay they remained at the old family home. It was here in 1875 that their first child, Mary, was born closely followed by five brothers and three sisters.

The cottage at Hopehead is now ruinous but in Jimmy's time it stood near the burn and was the usual pattern with a byre on one end. They soon left Kingledores and Jimmy became a herd at Oliver and the family moved into Oliver Cottage which stood on the triangle between the Moffat Road, the road to Carlowes Bridge and the old

Mr and Mrs Millar (Mary Kerr Brown).

toll road. This was much nearer the school and more convenient for the growing family. Jimmy was a herd at Oliver for 30 years and even after he retired he continued to take a great interest in the farm. Oliver Cottage is now in ruins but some years ago one of his grandchildren, for sentimental reasons, bought the triangle including the old ruin.

Many tales were told of old Jimmy: his knowledge of sheep, his skill with the leister (especially at clodding), his prodigious memory, ability to narrate stories, skill in writing verse, some satirical and political (he was an enthusiastic Tory) and his sense of humour. He earned the respect of a wide circle of friends. His comment 'aye laddie, ye can clod', when I successfully used the leister to catch him a salmon, was one of the highlights of my youth.

None of James' sons remained in Tweedsmuir. John emigrated to America and became a sheep farmer in Sun Valley, Tom emigrated to Canada, William became a chief inspector in the Glasgow police, Jim herded and eventually managed Drumelzier Place. Alec was killed in the Great War. He had been the postman and delivered over the hills from Tweed to Fruid, Menzion and Talla by foot. I have a very early memory of him running and winning the hill race in 1911. The daughters apart from Mary all married locally.

Mary was a star pupil at the Tweedsmuir school and when she was due to leave Dominie Brown (no relation) was keen that she should stay on and continue her education for an extra year. Jimmie would

The Riggs.

Bell Shaw at the Riggs.

not entertain the idea and, at twelve years old, she had to leave like the rest of the pupils.

As a rule girls leaving school became domestic servants, often in local houses. Farmers had at least two domestics, as did the Ministers, while the lairds and other large establishments needed larger numbers. Mary Brown ventured far from home to Ayrshire and then to Inverary Castle. She then went to Algiers with Lady Arthur where she became fluent in French.

Back in Scotland Mary was employed by Lady Coats of the famous cotton firm from Paisley. She was now involved with secreterial work

The Riggs, with Bell Shaw in background.

connected with the Tory party, which incidentally her father had favoured all his life. She never lost touch with her now elderly parents and frequently travelled to Tweedsmuir to visit them.

It was at this time that the construction of the Talla dam and reservoir was in progress and Mary sometimes came out from

Broughton on the small railway built to carry materials to the site. While working in Glasgow she met an engineer and in 1905 she married him and became Mrs Millar. Their eldest daughter, Margaret was to become my wife half a century later. Jimmie Brown died in January 1925 aged 78 and his wife Margaret two years later aged 77 years.

Recollections of people and events are passed on by way of the written and spoken word. Sometimes it is the remains of the past which awaken these recollections. Take for example the old Talla railway. Practically all that now remains to be seen of this once imporatnt line are the tall concrete pillars of the sheep over-bridges. A few were blown up for practice by army engineers in the 1939–45 war. A characteristic of the railway was the number of crossings and footbridges which connected the land on both sides. On Mossfennan alone there were four level crossings (each with two heavy iron gates) and five over bridges. In addition there were several substantial culverts, mainly over burns. The one large aquaduct to carry the pipes across the Tweed at Glenriskie is one landmark that will not be removed.

The trains ceased to run as soon as the dam was officially opened but it took a few years to dismantle the railway lines and sleepers. As children we could always find discarded triangular shovels. The fences along the railway line remained intact and in good condition for many years and John Watt, the supervisor at the dam, ran a small flock of sheep which had access to the grazing right down to Rachan. When he needed to gather them he took one of his sons to Rachan in his De Dion Boulton car (one of the first cars in the area) and walked with the collected sheep back to Talla.

Unlike the railway, the cottages situated about a mile above Tweed-smuir on the Moffat road have completely disappeared. Here two almost identical cottages, known as the Riggs, stood on the right of the road, at the boundary between Oliver and Glenbreck. Some three hundred yards further up the same boundary, but on the old road, once stood a single shepherd's house now long since abandoned. The last occupant was James Brown's grandfather. Near it across the Riggs burn can be seen the outline of a still older dwelling and its dry stone was probably used to buld the other house or the march wall.

The two cottages on the new road were of simple 'but and ben' construction, and quite primitive. Water was obtained from a spring on the opposite side of the road or from the nearby burn. The lower cottage had a garden with a stone wall round it and was occupied by a very old retired herd, Jamie Anderson. The other cottage was a little higher and was occupied by an old and very colourful character known as Bell Shaw. Old Jamie had quite well-to-do relations but Bell had only a son who lived some distance away.

Jamie was the first to pass away but Bell stayed on at her lonely cottage. She kept a few hens which were allowed to use one end of the house but quite often visited both compartments. By now she was quite blind and relied on neighbours for help. The young herd from Glenbreck visited most days and brought her water and fuel but it was always a wonder that she kept going. The old age pension at that time was half a crown a week (12½p) and she must have found life very difficult.

At last her son managed to persuade her to move. All the folk in Tweedsmuir came out to wave her goodbye. Swathed in rugs and blankets and wearing an unfamiliar hat, Bell climbed into her son's motorbyke and side car and left her familiar surroundings and feathered friends. Within a few weeks she had passed away.

Her cottage was the first to be demolished but the other remained for several years and was occupied at weekends by boys from an Edinburgh school. About 1993 a heavy truck left the road and crashed into the remaining cottage and left it uninhabitable. It was then levelled to the ground. The third generation of the Riggs is now no more noticable than the first which existed three or four hundred years ago.

I have attempted to give some account of the Upper Tweed Valley as I remember it. Official records can only provide the skeleton of the history of a community and I hope that my recollections may add some of the flesh, bones and soul which keep the past alive. Time passes quickly and all too soon people, places and events have gone and are forgotten as though they had never been.

Appendix One *Poems*

These two poems and notes were among Andrew Lorimer's papers.

While most of the larger farms employed several married shepherds, they also had a 'young herd' who could be a school leaver or a much older person who had stayed on in one place without getting married. For a young herd the transition to the status of a married man with his own animals and the responsibility of a larger flock was an important step in his career. The verses below, written in the Lallans of the nineteenth century, give some indication of life in an 'oot bye' herding:

THE PROPOSAL

Noo Jeanie a hae some news for ye,
news a'm fair fain tae tell
but it isna news for spreedin
it's a secret for yersel.

A've a chance tae tak a herding
up a a bonny Border glen
wi' a canty wee bit biggin
though its juist a but an ben.

An although it's bielded frae the blast
it gets its share o' sun
frae early in the mornin'
till the day is gie weel run.

On yae side there's a kail yaird
Wi' a burnie runnin' by,
on the ither stands the hey shed
an' a byre for twae three kye.

An' at the back the kennel,
a hen hoose and a sty,
an' in the front a sturdy rowan tree
grows stoot an' straucht an' high.

Inside a cosy box bed

stands next the ingle neuk,
an' the fire-place has a swee
wi' a chain an' chimney heuk.

There's cleiks up in the kipples
for hams and reestd fish,
sae oo'l hae fare a plenty
as ony yin could wish.

There's a wee square gable windae
looks up a fernie ghill
where ye can see me comin'
wi' ma doggies frae the hill.

An' a'll ken afore a' lift the sneck
the welcome waits for me,
the softness o' yere willin' lips
an' the love licht in yere ee.

Oh Jeanie, it wad brek ma hairt,
ye winna say me nay,
an' a'll gang an' gie oor cries
an' ye can set the day.

The 'wee square gable windae' was a common feature in many cottages.
A good example can still be seen at Badlieu, on the road to Moffat.
The rowan tree is significant as few couples in those times would have
cared to defy the superstition and occupy a dwelling which was unprotected by the magical properties of the venerated rowan tree.

GLOSSARY

Canty	cheerful
Biggin	building
Cleiks	hooks
Kipples	rafters
Reested	dried, salted and half-smoked.
Sneck	latch
Cries	banns, called three times on different Sundays

FURNISHING

Oo'l need a hantle plenishin'
although the hoose is wee
an' an unco lot o' hoose gear
that ye better ken than me.

Oo'l need a new-made girnel
tae haud baith meal an' flour,
a knock abune the mantlepiece
tae wairn us o' the oor.

An' a'll order a braw dresser
wi' drawers an' a shelf
whaure yer can keep yere cheeny
an' shaw yere bonny delft.

But a'll hae tae see the banker
for a've a guid wheen pence laid by
for a heifer for the byre
an' a grumphie for the sty.

Then oo'l mak a veesit tae the toon
for the most important thing
for sen eev kept ma token safe
oo'l change it for the ring.

An' on the day ye hansel it
as proud a man oo'l be
as any lord or prince or king
in the hale o' Kirsendie.

Mind ye, oo'l no be idle
till the peats and hey are won
an' oo'l work in God's guid caller air
aneath the summer sun.
An' whan the peat stack's high and theeked,
the hayshed dasses fou,
oo'l ken that oo hae provender
tae see the winter through.

In the outlying hirsels the newly married couple had to provide food
for themselves and their animals as well as fuel for the whole year,

hence the reference to peats and hay. The word 'knock' (clock) was still used when I was a boy. The dresser was a most important piece of furniture and the pattern could vary with the requirements of the user. These dressers were handmade by local craftsmen whose individual designs and work were easily recognisable. The 'token' mentioned would certainly not have been a ring which then a mark of married status. The 'token' could be almost anything and was often kept a secret between the couple. Items that could be halved often featured as tokens, such as 'the crooked bawbee' (halfpenny), half a sixpence, pages of the Bible, even a Valentine. All these signified the intention to marry. The word 'fiancée' was unknown and 'intended' was the usual expression. The practice of 'Hand-Fasting' (to betroth by joining hands in order to cohabit before marriage) seems to have disappeared or is seldom used in the Borders.

GLOSSARY

Hantle	a fair amount
Unco	unknown
Girnel	meal ark, a container with compartments to separate flour and oatmeal
Haud	hold
Knock	clock
Grumphie	sow
Hansel	wear for the first time
Kirstendie	Christendom
Caller	fresh
Theeked	thatched

I   THE FIDDLER

In one respect at least Tweedsmuir benefited from the upheaval caused by the building of the Talla dam. When the last of the work was completed and the personnel, except for the maintenance staff, had all departed, one important relict remained – the wooden village hall. No longer needed as a temporary building at Talla, it had been re-erected at the junction of the Moffat road with the new road. A new dimension was added to the social life of the district as concerts and dances could now be held. Whist drives and carpet bowling soon followed. One development, almost unique to Tweedsmuir, was the advent of the combined whist drive and dance which catered for all ages and most tastes.

Music for dancing was provided by fiddlers of whom there was no shortage as nearly every household had a violin and some families were especially gifted musically. For many years both before and after the Great War two fiddlers, Will Brown and Willie Todd, were the main providers of dance music. Willie was small and slight, and although he served at the front during the First World War for a short time, he was not fit for heavy work. He had violin lessons, became a very proficient player and lived to a great age.

Will on the other hand was robust, fond of life and of an occasional dram. He played entirely by ear and provided first-class dance music. Amplifiers were unknown in those days, so when more volume was needed Will could 'lay on the bow and gie it laldy'. He too had served in the forces during the war and had worked at Oliver and Talla. When he became ill with cancer he had to give up work at the dam and went to live at the Toll. Here he kept himself mobile by going for walks, but as he became progressively weaker, it was only with a great effort that he could walk down to Carlowes Brig and back.

One morning he met a gaun body (tramp) at the Brig with what looked like a fiddle in the bag he was carrying over his shoulder. He was indeed a busker who played at shows, fairs and other events and, taking his fiddle from its bag, he entertained his fellow violinist with a tune or two. Will was in his element and enquired if the busker could play 'The Laird o' Dunblair'. On hearing the tune, which was new to Will, he asked if the tramp would 'come away up tae the hoose till a get the fingering o't'. At Will's slow pace they climbed the slope to the Toll. Will soon had the fingering, as he called it, and mastered the tune with its distinctive beat. The two spent much of the day playing their repertoires, brothers in the art of music-making.

'The Laird o' Dunblair' was the last tune Will learned. Although only in his forties, his health rapidly declined but he still played his fiddle, latterly sitting up in bed. On his last morning on earth he asked his wife to bring him his fiddle and he played his favourite tunes including 'The Laird o' Dunblair'. Completely exhausted, he laid down his fiddle and bow for the last time.

At one time Will fell out with the Minister and stopped attending the Kirk. A local worthy, considering his arrival on 'the other side', is said to have remarked: 'Mind ye, he didna aye agree we the Minister, an' if he gangs up a dinna think he'll tak tae the herp but if he gangs doon – man, man – he'll gie auld nick a richt guid tune on the fiddle'. A fitting epitaph to a musician who, when the occasion arose, knew well how to 'lay on wi' the bow an gie it laldy'.

2   THE WHITE CATS OF OVER MENZION

The hirsel of cheviot sheep that occupied the head waters of Menzion was herded from a cottage called Over Menzion. In this context 'Over' was the equivalent of 'Upper Menzion' but in most other similar situations 'Hopehead' would be used, as at Stanhope Hopehead and Kingledores Hopehead and many others. These isolated herdings were often taken by young shepherds as their first job as married men. They did not expect to remain there permanently, and when their children reached school age they would move to more accessible situations. Sometimes older shepherds came there when their families had grown up, but few stayed for more than five or six years.

One shepherd who lived there just after the First World War had white cats which were left behind when he moved. From then onward white cats became a feature of the house, covering the time of several occupants and generations of cats. White cats seem to be quite common now but at that time the Over Menzion felines were the only ones of their kind in Tweedsmuir. As these cats were so far from other cats, they did not breed regularly, but with their reputation as good hunters there was never any difficulty in finding homes for any surplus kittens.

This story is about an old cat and her one remaining kitten. One day in midwinter a severe snowstorm had started and was threatening to continue, so the shepherd made his round with particular care to make sure he had all his own flock and to put any Talla Garelet sheep back on their own ground. The shepherd was checking part of the flock on the ridge of the Garelet, overlooking Talla reservoir, when his dogs chased a hare over the edge and killed it. Collies are not good retrievers, and as the snow was so deep and the ground so steep, the hare had to be left. This was at least a mile and a half from Over Menzion. The shepherd called his dogs up, continued homeward and thought no more of the incident.

Next morning, soon after daybreak, the herd's wife called him to a back window which looked up the hill towards Talla. There, halfway down the steep slope, came the old cat dragging the carcass of the abandoned hare through the snow. Evidently the dogs had carried enough scent to arouse the old cat's instincts sufficiently to inspire her to backtrack the dogs' trail. She then dragged the load, as heavy as herself, the long mile and a half home to her kitten.

With modern land use Over Menzion has long been abandoned. The land is now enveloped in a thick green mantle of Sitka Spruce and there are no more opportunities for resourceful and intelligent cats, white or otherwise.

3   JOHN FRENCH AND THE PARTRIDGES

John French herded a hirsel at the head of Fruid which extended from the foot of Carterhope Burn to the top of Hartfell. It was bounded on one side by the Fruid Burn and on the Carterhope side by a march dyke. His cottage, Nether Fruid, is now under the waters of the reservoir. When I knew John he must have been in his late sixties – still straight, tall and handsome. He was a most reliable herd who knew every inch of the ground he herded. He could direct one anywhere on his beat with complete accuracy and also had great knowledge of the wildlife of the area. The hirsel itself had some interesting features including the Spoot Heids, a series of waterfalls in a deep and narrow gorge, the Hawk Linn waterfall and the Craigie Middens, a heap of large, flattish pieces of rock piled up under a huge rock from which they had been gouged by frost.

He talked about the difference there was between fox control in his day and now. Every year before lambing time he had to make sure 'no ower mony foxes were aboot'. When the lambs started to arrive and the birds began to sit on their eggs, the foxes would take both to feed their cubs. 'Noo a days folk gang aboot things in a gey different way. They can afford tae wait till a wheen (number of) lambs hae been killed then they wait up wi' lichts an' shoot the auld foxes wi' rifles but they dinnae even ken where the cubs are or whether they dee o' hunger or no. Then, of coorse, oo had tae hae the foxes afore they cubbed'.

One of John's stories was about a severe winter snowstorm. 'Efter the big storm a' the howes were that fou o' snow that the drifts lested for weeks an weeks an it was then a' saw a sicht ai'd never seen in a ma herdin' life. A' wis gaun tae the hill yae mornin' an' a' was passin a big wreath o' hard snow at the back o' the Knocks, whan ma young doug gaed doon the brae an' stude settin' at the edge o' the drift. A' thocht it micht be a hare but he wadna leave it sae a' gaed doon tae see what he was at. Dae ye ken what it was – a wheen o' wee paitricks (covey of partridges) a' frosted together. Ye ken a gloutin o' wet snow haed faen in the middle o' the nicht an' the wee craturs had a' been a' cooried thegither in a boorick [shepherd's hut] for heat in the lee o' the drift an' whan the frost cam the hard coatin' kept them stuck thegither. Whan a' broke the ice wi' ma stick yin or twae got free but they couldna flee for the ice on their backs. Mind ye a' thocht o' fellin' yin takin' it hame for ma denner but a' couldna bring masel tae herm the gem [pretty] wee things. They're a' safe an' nane the waur for a've seen them since, the same half dizzen, sae oo'l hav a nest or twae as usual come the simmer.'

4   THE HORNED CHEVIOT

Fashion, so often associated with the word fickle or changeable, exerts powerful influences in many facets of life, even farming life. Many years age horns became unfashionable on the heads of Cheviot sheep so, for generations, they were so bred that few were to be seen even with the stubs which indicated their ancestral appearance. Occasionally, however, nature produced individuals with the horned characteristics so that there were always a few tups to carry horns to another generation. For example, on the two Cheviot hirsels at Hearthstane there was only one horned specimen while on Menzion, with three hirsels, there were none at all. Nowadays the horned variety has staged a comeback.

This is an anecdote about that horned Cheviot tup at Hearthstane. With the advantage of the unique weaponry at his disposal it is not surprising that he learned to lord it over his companions. An incident in his career is told in the words of the shepherd. 'When tup time cam roond, he went oot tae a heft where he was a' by himsel' and he was nae bather for the first ten days or sae. But yae mornin' he was on anither heft ai-tue- gether an a' had tae get him back tae his un yowes. Whan a' tried tae shed him off he chased the doug for its life an' that g'ie'd me the chance tae get in between him an' the rest o' the sheep. But he just put his heid doon an' cam straucht at i' like an express train. A' had tae jamp oot o' his way an' he just missed ma leg but he got ma stick an' it broke like a pipe stapple (stalk of a tobacco pipe). O'e couldna leave him there sae a' kept at him wi' ma twae dougs an' the bit o' stick a' had left. It took a long time for he aye faced up tae the dougs but there was twae o' them an' he began tae get richt tired. Whan he saw he was bate (beat) he turned roon wi' his heid in the air an' trotted away back whir he cam frae an' never even looked ower his shooder. O'aye, it didna cure him – he still was inclined tae raik (roam) but he was a lot easier tae han'le frae then on.

5   BRAXY SHEEP

In times not so long past braxy (diseased) mutton was a regular part of the winter diet of the hill herds and their families. This gastric infection sometimes proved fatal so quickly that the meat was seriously tainted soon after the demise of the unfortunate victim. If the infected animal could be slaughtered and thoroughly bled and cleaned, the flesh was perfectly good to eat. Suitably salted and dried, it would keep for months, making a welcome addition to the often meagre household fare. One problem, however, always faced the shepherd – had he diagnosed correctly and should he slaughter the animal at once, or wait to see if it might recover? This dilemma faced a certain herd one late autumn morning, as the following story shows.

'A' was coming in frae the hill yae mornin' an' Samuel was comon' doon the ither side o' the burn at the same time. He shouted across but a' couldna hear for the burn so a' guid doon tae the burnside an' he cam doon on his side tae. He had an ailin' hogg in the back stell and wasna shair whither it was braxy or no an' he wanted me tae hae a look at it wi' him after denner time.

After a'd had ma denner a' went wi' him tae the stell away up the back burn. The beast was deid but warm eneuch tae bleud, sae oo' bled it an' set about skinnin an' gutten it. It was a kind o' rouch job an' Samuel's knife must hae slippit for the bag was cut an' the hale lot splashed a' ower the place. It was an awfy mess an' an awfy smell. Hoo-ever oo' got the maist o't scraped off but it was far frae clean so a' said tae him that it was no very nice for takin' tae the weemen folk. Didn'e he think oo' should maybe gee it a bit wash? 'Man', says he, 'that's what's wrang we' folk noo adays. They're far ower denty feeders.'

Nevertheless oo' gied it a guid wash in the burn an' made it a wee bit mair respectable. When oo' got hame he cut it up an' a' had tae tak a leg hame wi' me. Whan oo' ete it a' couldn'a help thinkin' o' Samuel an' his 'denty feeders'. That was a lang time back but the ether day a' read in the paper that experts, doctors, have just fund oot that what's wrang wi' folk noo adays is they're far ower denty feeders. But Samuel was nae doctor – juist an auld herd.'

6   BRAID LAW (BROAD LAW)

Our highest hill, Braid Law or Broad Law, is a broad, rounded mass with ridges running outwards in all directions and with burns which carry water to Megget and Tweed. At 2,756 feet it fails by over 200 feet to attain Munro status. A huge gash on the north face, Polmood Craig, consists of exposed rock and scree and looks down on an area of deep peat hags. The upper heights are covered with short, stunted heather, mosses and even lichen. In winter the top of the craig fills with a big moon-shaped drift of deep snow which hardens with frost and sometimes lasts until June.

Sometimes snowstorms ended in lan-drift – drifting snow at ground level – which curled over the top and formed a great snow cornice which curved all round the top of the craig. The hill foxes saw the great cornice as a shelter and a place of safety. One shepherd found himself up under the cornice but had lost his nerve on the hard, icy drift. Luckily he had a trapper's spade with him and this enabled him to cut a hole upwards which eventually came out on the top of the overhanging snow.

The end of November and the month of December can often provide wide variations of weather conditions. One year James (Jimmy) Brown, who was born at Kingledores Hopehead and herded Oliver for nearly half a century, experienced some unusual weather on Broad Law. This occurred at tup time which, with lambing, is perhaps one of the most important and the most testing of a shepherd's skill. When Jimmy heard people complaining about bad weather at that time of year, he would recount one of his own experiences.

'A' was juist a bit hauflen at the time, maybe fifteen or sixteen. The herd at Hearthstane had turned no weel richt afore tup time and a' was sent tae tak his place. Of course a' didn'a ken the tups or the ground but wi' the man next door o'o got them out an' on their hefts only a day or twae late, an' there were fower o' them hefts.

Braid Law herdin' has the widest boonds an the highest green in the country. It had been a grand back en' an' the sheep were strong an' wild an' runnin' high oot. O'o got the tups oot tae the hefts a'a richt but in a day or twae hard wather cam in we' frost an' the thickest mist a've ever seen. Ye expect tae coont a'a the hefts every mornin' in tup time but mornin' efter mornin' ther was nae a sheep tae be seen. But they were there for a' could aye hear the dunner (noise) o' their feet on the hard grund. Dugs were na much guid. A' had yen o' ma ain an' yen o' the herd's but it was lettle yuis for it didna want tae work for me, an' onyway the sheep paid nae attention tae them in the mist.

This gaed on richt tae Christmas an' a' had never managed tae coont the hefts let alone see if the tups were in their places. Whan the weather cleared it was time for the tups tae come in an' maist were wantin' hame onyway. O'o aa' thocht it wad be a fair disaster we' an awfy lot o' yeld [barren] yowes an' a' was fair feared o' lambing time. Hoo wrang a body can be! There was hardly a yeld yowe. The mist, ee see, had keepit the hefts separate an' the tups had stayed where they were puit'.

7   GAUN BODIES OR GANGRELS (TRAMPS)

Some years ago it was not uncommon to see gaun bodies or gangrels on our country roads. Not all were beggars and many worked for their food and shelter. At Tweedsmuir a small house on Menzion Knows was maintained to provide these wanderers with shelter. When the Poor Law changed, the house was pulled down and vagrants were allowed shelter at Menzion. Most were taciturn and sometimes unpleasant, but there were exceptions, and some regulars appeared at the same time each year because of the availability of work.

At old Stanhope Bridge, on land alongside the Talla railway, a collection of great iron pipes lay neatly arranged and ready for use if any bursts occurred where the water, on its way to Edinburgh, ran in pipes after it left the tunnels. These huge pipes, four or five feet in diameter, made good sleeping quarters for the travelling tramps. When one end was partly closed to reduce draughts and bracken or old clothes were packed in, these pipes became quite comfortable and much frequented by many kinds of gaun bodies.

One day a couple with a bright young baby in a pram arrived at Mossfennan. Perhaps the sight of the baby sucking away at a bottle of cold tea and laughing with satisfaction made my wife decide to allow them to stay. They camped in a wood near the roadside and were able to light a fire. As frequently happened, a good lamb had been killed on the then unfenced road and I gave it to them.

Instead of leaving the next day, the couple asked if they might do some work. I had turnips needing to be singled and it took some time to teach them the art. They were keen to learn and eventually managed the task, but not very well. When the neeps were finished they left. In the autumn we were surprised to receive a phone call from near Inverness asking if the turnips were ready for shawing. We could hardly refuse, and in a few days John and Janet had arrived. This pattern continued for a year or two.

Sometime later we had a strange message from Saughton gaol. It was from John. Their condition had deteriorated, they had been drinking Red Biddy and had been taken into custody. By now they had two little children. My wife and I had never been in a gaol before and Saughton was most forbidding. We finished up bailing them both out into the care of the authorities who would unite Janet and the children, if it were thought advisable.

One cold, stormy night about two years later John came back to Mossfennan. My wife and I were out somewhere and we didn't know he was there until the next morning when he arrived at the back door shivering with cold. He had spent the night, wet and miserable, in a cold shed. My wife put him in the boiler room and brought him fresh clothes. With some good food he recovered, and when he was given one of my discarded overcoats he remarked that he felt like a gentleman. He had come to tell us that he and Janet had separated. She was in a mental home and the children were in care. John himself then left to go south and we never heard from him again.

Appendix Three *A Village School in Wartime*

In 1938 Andrew Lorimer was appointed headmaster of Whitekirk school in East Lothian and remained there until 1946 when problems with his voice prevented him from continuing his teaching career. He was very keen that there should be some record of life in this rural village during the Second World War, centred on the village school. When he wrote this account almost 45 years later he noted: 'Unfortunately I have to make the circumstances and explanations in a personal vein'.

A VILLAGE SCHOOL IN WARTIME

In 1938 I was appointed headmaster of the small rural school at Whitekirk in East Lothian. The village, about four miles from North Berwick, had a population of some 750 and consisted of two lines of cottages facing each other with a road between. A new schoolhouse had just been built on high ground at the top of the village and I was its first occupant. It stood in part of a grass paddock with a high brick wall behind as a protection against the prevailing winds. Once quick-growing hedges of lonicera (honeysuckle) had been planted and turf laid, the house and garden soon took on quite a respectable appearance.

The house was bungalow-style and quite commodious. One room acted as an office and, as headmasters were traditionally also the local Registrars, it contained a large safe for registration books and documents. The school roll numbered 50 primary pupils, most of whom would leave at 12 when they qualified for the High School at North Berwick. Those who failed stayed on until leaving age.

My assistant, Mrs Pattison, had taught at the school for most of her working life and lived in the Old Schoolhouse with her elderly mother. Her knowledge of the people was invaluable, especially as she was Secretary and Treasurer of the Women's Rural Institute (WRI).

On taking over the school, my methods and attitude, as expected, differed from those of my predecessor. He had retired after many years' service and latterly, with his health and energy failing, pupils had taken advantage of opportunities to misbehave. Discipline had been upset and pranks, such as changing the time on the clock to get away early, were not uncommon.

Whitekirk School, 1946. Classes 5, 6 and 7. (*Mr W Guthrie*)

Back row (left to right): M Clark, W Guthrie, G Chalmers, S Jarvis, J Masterton, F Anderson, D Keir, T Main, R Graham, P Gordon, G White, D Clark, C McDougall

Middle row (left to right): H Stewart, M Anderson, I Howden, J Scott, M Main, J Hastings, M Hume, A Scott, G Graham, I Blair, D Bathgate. (Mr Lorimer, Headmaster)

Front row (left to right): M Stewart, W Hume, E Masterton, J White, B Reid, H McDougall, H Scott, M Johnston.

One pupil had been at about half-a-dozen schools because of his disruptive behaviour. Before I came he had been let out of school half-an-hour early to avoid trouble on the way home. I had to be a bit severe with him and always dealt with him on a one-to-one basis until we understood each other. He eventually adapted to the school's regime and at 12 passed his qualifying examination to the High School.

War was looming and in September 1939 came the great upheaval with the evacuation of children from the cities. I was appointed billeting officer, and between 20 and 30 children of mixed ages arrived from Edinburgh. It was difficult to get accommodation for them all locally, so several were taken to houses in Tyninghame village nearby. The enlarged school roll with so many pupils without country experience or knowledge made our work very difficult. Some evacuees were frightened and homesick, while others adapted and enjoyed the rural life. With no air raids a proportion drifted back to Edinburgh. Among those who remained a few became almost countryfied.

Air Raid Wardens had to be appointed and a Home Defence Unit (later called the Home Guard) was formed. At first I was a member of both but when there was the possibility of gas being used I became responsible for gas training and left the Home Guard.

As the war proceeded the whole community and especially our school became involved in the war effort. Manufacturers of certain medicines made from wild plants became short of raw materials. We found that many of the medicinal plants needed grew nearby and we were sent lists of instructions of what was required and how to collect and dry them. Soon the school was festooned with drying leaves and, with Mrs Pattison's help, the Rural Hall was also made available. This increased the scale of our activity and farmers lent us wire netting to sling across the hall. When we needed sacks, they provided them and also arranged transport of the dried plants to the railway station.

Mrs Pattison had a very interesting old copy of Culpepper's book on medicinal herbs and medicines. It contained hundreds of recipes for cures using plants or parts of plants found in the countryside. The plants we were gathering were all mentioned in the book with details for their preparation and use as medicines.

My memory of all the plants is far from perfect but I recall long lines of coltsfoot leaves strung up to dry, with care being taken to keep them away from direct sunlight which destroyed the potency of the leaves. Burdock was another leaf we also collected. One of the most valuable in terms of money was foxglove seed (digitalis), but it was difficult to collect even in ounces.

In some other plants the roots were required. Amongst these was malefern and another with thick, almost tuberous roots which we found on the banks of the nearby River Tyne. Meadowsweet was also wanted, and even broom which had to be collected in fullest bloom. The enthusiasm of the children sometimes involved the older members of their families. One Saturday morning I was working in my garden when a horse and cart with two of my pupils pulled up opposite. It was loaded high with newly cut broom. Workers on a nearby estate had been cutting down some rampant broom and the children had cajoled their big brother into fetching the fresh branches to add to our store.

The war came when rural conditions were still in the shadow of the hungry 'thirties and many children in country schools were under-nourished. In certain seasons of the year both parents would be working with the women in lines of up to 20 singling (thinning) turnips or swedes. As cold winds were common, sweeping across the exposed fields, they wore a type of stiff, lightweight hood which protected their faces. In summer these hoods, called 'uglies', gave protection from too much sun. At night, when the children returned from school, they had to fend for themselves until their mothers returned from work. Wartime shortages and rationing aggravated the low diet and there were several families showing signs of poor nutrition.

Children would come to school with 'pieces' that were so unappetising that they couldn't finish them. The sugar shortage meant that jam could not be made and the butter ration soon ran out. Even though we provided cocoa, the dry, unspread pieces remained half-eaten. Brambles, which some of the mothers once gathered to make into jelly with crab apples, were now untouched though plentiful. The missing ingredient was sugar.

So Whitekirk School registered as a jam factory and I obtained a permit to buy sugar in some quantity. The effect was immediate. Children came to school with brambles in every type of container and bags of crab apples. Most of the work of making our product was done in the schoolhouse by my wife who had plenty of experience in making jam, or in this case jelly. Jars, mostly 2lbs size, were brought to us and when filled were stored at the school. If I remember correctly, a form had to be completed to show that the precious sugar had been used properly.

The results of our efforts soon became apparent and were most satisfactory. To make sure that the jam would not run out we used it for three days each week when we would spread it liberally on the pupils' bread. Parents found it easier to provide for the other days, so it suited both them and the children. The fact that they had helped to provide their own food had quite a good effect on the morale and atmosphere of our little school. Eventually school meals were provided but the jam factory had carried us through the time of greatest need.

The appeal for dog-hips to make into the vitamin-rich rose hip syrup brought such a response that our contribution far outstripped that of the other schools in the county. The appeal for scrap metal was equally successful but much of it was so heavy that it had to be collected at the farms.

When the War Savings Scheme came into action, a sympathetic

farmer lent me his little run-about car. This enabled me to travel round the district fairly late in the evenings when families were all at home. My assistant, Mrs Pattison, accompanied me to help with issuing the certificates. Many people and children had been saving money in tins and bottles in such quantities that it took ages to count the coins and issue the stamps and certificates. By the second year amounts rose and we had to issue bonds for larger denominations than were allowed for certificates. Small coins were favourites among the children who would produce their containers full of 3d bits or 6d pieces and obtain their own savings stamps or certificates. Though most contributors were poorly paid farm workers, our results were extremely satisfactory. As there were no parent/teacher associations in those days, the Savings Scheme gave us an unexpected bonus with invaluable contact being made between us and the parents and older members of the families.

As Registrar of Births, Marriages and Deaths the country school-master met members of the community at important times or even crises in their lives. Whitekirk was no exception. In addition the village was near the training aerodrome at East Fortune and a long shoreline dotted with land mines. Deaths through crashes and mine explosions on both sea and land were registered at the schoolhouse. Bereaved individuals were usually glad of a little help with unfamiliar formalities and procedures and probably found the 'dominie' (schoolmaster) more approachable than a strange official behind a counter.

My duties as an Air Raid Warden included attending night-flying accidents and recording any bombs that were dropped. One tragic accident occurred when some German prisoners of war, who had been working in the area, walked into a coastal minefield when taking a shortcut on the way back from work. Several were killed instantly and others died on their way to hospital. It was difficult to obtain the proper facts until the official documents came from the military auth-orities.

A decoy lay-out not far from the village attracted only one attack by enemy planes. The bluff must have been detected as they never returned, although the lights were switched on and off for some time. A mine dropped on a hill behind East Linton shook up the houses at Whitekirk although the distance must have been at least three miles.

Events in aid of the Red Cross were held in the WRI Hall opposite the schoolhouse, so we were always involved. These were usually whist drives and sometimes there were a few hours' dancing afterwards. It was often difficult to provide food for these occasions. Sandwiches were always the main item and the filling was usually rabbit. The local rabbit catcher always knew when one of these events was to take place and would leave a pair of good rabbits at the schoolhouse. These we made into a spreading pâte, and to vary the flavour additives such as Bovril would be used in the mixture.

Music for the dancing came from an accordion and the WRI piano. Sometimes we had a competition. The Old Time Waltzes were usually won by a middle-aged couple whose timing and perfect footwork indicated a long addiction to the 'light fantastic'.

Concerts were difficult to organise as locals were too shy to perform in public, so we had to look for outside talent. A youth club was started which consisted entirely of boys. The lack of facilities was a great disadvantage and the club only just managed to survive.

Unfortunately Andrew Lorimer never completed this account of Whitekirk school during the war and his notes end rather abruptly. Although he describes a period of his life away from the Upper Tweed Valley, it is interesting to note the great influence his life in that area had upon the activities of Whitekirk school and how much his pupils would have learned from his wide knowledge of the countryside and of human nature.

Appendix Four   *The Tweedsmuir Curling Club*

The records of the Tweedsmuir Curling Club are contained in two well-worn books. The first, entitled 'School Exercises', covers the period 1860–1871 and the second carries on until 1925. The latter has been repaired and reinforced with fine cord to hold the pages together in place of the thread which had evidently worn out. The back of this book is embellished with a framed representation of a ship, a Man of War, in full sail. The initial headings in both books were written by the then schoolmaster, Dominie Brown, in the most perfect cursive form, and though the ink has faded the style is a joy to behold.

There seems to have been some curling on the site before the formation of the club. As at Broughton, whose club had existed since 1816, the Tweedsmuir curlers owed the foundation of their club to the initiative of their Minister, the Revd John Dick, who called the inaugural meeting on December 27, 1860 with 16 curlers present. John Carruthers of Fruid was elected 'Preses', the old Scots term, though by 1864 the title 'President' was in use. A full set of rules was drawn up and orders were given for the pond to be enlarged. The subscription for 1860 at 2/– (10p) attracted 29 members, of whom 24 were designated regular players. Six skips were appointed. Within a few years the roll rose to over 40 and the fee dropped to 1/– (5p).

On January 6, 1861 the Secretary received a formal note from the Minister, indicating that he had procured a medal for the Tweedsmuir Curling Club which should be played for as a rink trophy. He urged an early match. A thaw interfered with this game and also a challenge match against Broughton, but the following winter the medal was played for over a period of three days with six rinks competing. The match for the medal became the premier event of each season. Challenge matches were played against Broughton and other neighbouring clubs. In addition a variety of other games, such as Married v Unmarried, Left Side of Tweed v Right Side, Shavers v Non-Shavers, were often played.

A gold locket was donated by Alexander Fleming in 1866, though no official note of the gift appears in the minutes. This was played for by a single-handed points competition. It is interesting to note that at this time a junior competition, held for a pair of curling stones

Tweedsmuir Curling Club Medal, presented in 1861.
(*Above*: front. *Opposite*: back)

given by Mr Dick, was won by Tom Dempster. His family was associated with the club throughout its entire existence and especially with the care of the pond which constantly needed repair.

In 1868 Mr T. Stodart of Oliver became president, the schoolmaster

remained as secretary, as indeed did succeeding dominies, while the Revd John Dick was designated chaplain. The next season's play commenced on December 1 and continued until at least January 26, 1870 when a challenge match was played against Biggar on the Rachan pond. Each side had four rinks competing and the game lasted 5½ hours.

At the end-of-the-season dinner held at the Crook Inn, Mr Stodart entertained the company with a 'rhyming chronicle' which described the splendid final contest for the medal on December 7, 1869. Darkness came down as the game reached its exciting climax and Tom Dempster of Dykehead brought out a lighted lantern which he placed on the tee (the mark made in the ice towards which the stones are pushed). The game continued with ever-rising tension and the lantern, of course, played a most important role. The very last stone defeated the hitherto unbeaten holders of the trophy who, according to the chorus of verse 11, 'lang will remember the seventh o' December when Tam set his lantern doon on the tee'. The 'rhyming chronicle' makes most interesting reading and includes many names long associated with the district.

The Club minutes note that in October 1871 'a list of members was sent to the Secretary of the Royal Caledonian Curling Club'. This list, of 27 members and two honorary members, is the first reference to the Tweedsmuir Club's membership of that club.

In 1873 the memo for the season notes that the pond was thoroughly puddled (repaired with clay) in early November but there was 'only one day's curling the whole season'. Five years later, in 1878–79, the club had a bumper year, for in addition to the usual competitions Tweedsmuir played 11 away matches. Most were with neighbouring clubs, Broughton, Peebles, Biggar, Moffat and two opponents with less familiar names – Forest and Hutton. The players did well, for overall they gained 156 shots against losses of only 42, and an extra competition was held for a pair of handles donated by Mr Sinclair.

After a year with 'but one game', there were two with no play at all but in 1884, in addition to the medal and locket competitions, a whole list of other prizes and trophies were played for. These included curling stone handles (a regular donation from Mr Dick the Minister), Mrs Bertram's Kettle, Mr Hamilton's Cup and Mr Welsh's Flagon. The Archibald Medal was won by the captain of the Non-Shavers, T.T. Stodart. In addition Tweedsmuir won the Caledonian Club Medal by defeating Broughton.

In 1891 an impatient entry for December 25 notes 'curling today for the first time this season'. Thereafter entries continued regularly and covered the usual matches for the Medal, the Locket, a special Jubilee Medal, Shavers v Non-Shavers, Right Bank of Tweed v Left Bank and so on. On February 19, 1892 the temperature was 1 degree below zero, the 33 degrees of frost enabling five hours of curling to take place.

When the club stopped for the season the following day, they had played almost continuously for over eight weeks.

At the close-of-season dinner held at the Crook Inn on February 26, Mr Walter Stuart of Kingledores offered to erect a curling house near the pond. Mr Lindsay of Stanhope said he would provide a stove and Mr Gunn the fuel. Eight months later the 'Club House' was completed and at the Annual Meeting held on October 29 the building was formally handed over as a gift from Mr Stuart. The Minutes recorded the 'hearty thanks' of the members for the 'comfortable and substantial club house in which the club were assembled'.

Sadly the secretary died and John Yellowlees succeeded John Brown in the post. Though Mr Yellowlees wrote clear and well itemised minutes, the underlying enthusiasm behind some of Mr Brown's comments is missing. In 1897, however, the secretary gives a day-by-day account of play and describes conditions variously as 'ice weak and biassed', 'ice pretty good but rather weak and a soo's back between the hog score and the tee made scoring difficult'.

The finances of the club seem to have been satisfactory with credit balances varying between 6½d and just over £1. At one point in 1902 a concert in the school and a dance at the Bield raised £4 and the club was in clover.

Little of interest is recorded until 'no play 1914–1915', and it is noted that three members had joined the Army in 1915. After the war in 1919 it was 'unanimously agreed to withdraw from the Royal Caledonian Curling Club owing to our inability to raise the number of rinks and the difficulty of getting to the railway station'. Annual Meetings were no longer being held in the 'curling hoose', and in 1923 the windows were boarded up to prevent tramps from sheltering there.

The weather pattern seems to have changed by this time as a note states '1921–22–23 no games owing to absence of frost', and in 1923–24 there was still no curling through 'absence of ice'. An entry for 1925 indicates a balance of £3–0–10½d and the subscription fixed at 1/6d. The last entry was made on December 17 1925 when it was resolved that the Annual Meeting should be held in the first week of November and that the pond should be filled that week. After that 'blank' – not even a postscript - and so ends the record of the Tweedsmuir Curling Club, not officially closed but seemingly in a state of suspended animation.

Appendix Five   *Register of Upper Tweed Valley Sheep Marks, 1907*

PEEBLESSHIRE—

FARM	POST TOWN	OCCUPIER	KEEL
Broughton Place	Broughton	John Tudhope	Far rib
Cloverhill	Do.	A. C. Gairns	
Kilbucho Place	Biggar	John Muirhead	Across kidneys
Ratchill	Broughton	E. B. Masterton	Red near rib

PEEBLESSHIRE—

Drumelzier Haugh	Broughton	W. L. Dickson	Sword far hip
Drumelzier Place	Do.	William Aitken	Near rib
Do. Hope Carton Hirsel	Do.	Do.	Far rib
Kingledores, Twilt Hirsel	Do.	Captain Stewart	Pop near rib
Do. Bonshaw Hirsel	Do.	Do.	Pop far rib
Do. Hopehead Hirsel	Do.	Do.	
Stanhope, Hope Hirsel	Do.	W. F. Lindsay	Far sword
Do. East Side Hirsel	Do.	Do.	Near sword
Do. Lowend East Hirsel	Do.	Do.	Near rib
Do. do. West Hirsel	Do.	Do.	Far rib
Patervan, Upper Hirsel	Do.	Robert Renwick	Near rib
Do. Under Hirsel	Do.	Do.	Near hip
Do. Shepherd's Park	Do.	Do.	2 near rib keels

PARISH OF BROUGHTON

EAR DIAGRAMS		FAR HORN	NEAR HORN	BUIST	REMARKS
Far Ear	Near Ear				
Various		T	—	**T** far rib	
				A G far hip **A G** far rib, Hoggs	Cheviot Ewes part crossed (part has a hole in ear)
				M	
				M near rib	

PARISH OF DRUMELZIER

		D		**D** near rib	
		A		**A** near rib	
		A		**A** far rib	
			S	**S** near hip	
			S	**S** far rib	
			S	**S** near rib	
				W far rib	Burned across nose before 1905
				W near rib	Do.
				W far rib	Do.
				W far rib	Do.
		R		**R** near rib	
		R		**R** far rib	
		P P		**R** near hip	

PEEBLESSHIRE—

FARM	POST TOWN	OCCUPIER	KEEL
Earlshaugh	Moffat	Tom Welsh	Red far rib
Tweedshaws	Do.	Do.	Red near rib
Carterhope, Hope Hirsel	Broughton	Do.	Black near rib
Do. Low Hirsel	Do.	Do.	Black far rib
Crook	Do.	Andrew P. Braes	Red near rib
Fingland	Do.	Mr Scott	Far rib
Fruid, Brandsbrae Hirsel	Do.	Robert R. Haddow	Far rib
Do. Eastside Hirsel	Do.	Do.	Near rib
Do. Westside Hirsel	Do.	Do.	Far rib
Gameshope	Do.	James Thomson	Sword near side
Talla, Upper Hirsel	Do.	Do.	Across kidneys
Do. Lower Hirsel	Do.	Do.	2 pops near rib
Glenbreck	Do.	A. P. Paterson	Red pop far rib
Do. Riggs Hirsel	Do.	Do.	Red pop near rib
Hawkshaw, Lower Hirsel	Do.	David Lyell	Red near rib
Do. Upper Hirsel	Do.	Do.	Red near rib, & pop on hip
Hearthstane, Burn Hirsel	Do.	Wm. Thorburn	Pop blue near rib
Do. Broadlaw Hirsel	Do.	Do.	Pop blue far rib
Do. Westside Hirsel	Do.	Do.	Pop red near rib

PARISH OF TWEEDSMUIR

EAR DIAGRAMS		FAR HORN	NEAR HORN	BUIST	REMARKS
Far Ear	Near Ear				
		W		I W far rib	
		W		I W near rib	
			T W	W near rib	
			T W	W far rib	Blackfaced Ewes & Cross Lambs
		B		B near rib	
				S far rib	Cheviot stock
				H far rib	Do.
		R H		H near rib	
		R H		H far rib	
				T near rib	
				ⓣ far rib	
				ⓣ near rib	
			P	P near rib	Started to burn and buist with P in 1907
		P		P far rib	Do.
				L near rib	Cheviot stock
			D L	L near hip	Cheviot stock and part Blackfaced Blackfaced will be all away in 3 years
		H		W T near rib	
		H		W T far rib	
				W T near rib	Cheviot stock

PEEBLESSHIRE—

FARM	POST TOWN	OCCUPIER	KEEL
Hearthstane, Cockland Hirsel }	Broughton	Wm. Thorburn	Red far rib
Menzion	Do.	Simon Linton	Near rib
Do. Craiglaw Hirsel	Do.	Do.	Far rib
Do. Over Menzion Hirsel	Do.	Do.	Far rib
Oliver	Do.	Thos. T. Stodart	Sword far side
Badlieu, Upper Hirsel	Do.	R. Macdiarmid	Pop near hip
Do. Lower Hirsel	Do.	Do	Pop far hip
Tweedhopefoot Hirsel	Do.	Do.	Pop far hip
Glencragie Hirsel	Do.	Do.	Long keel near rib

PARISH OF TWEEDSMUIR—*continued*

EAR DIAGRAMS		FAR HORN	NEAR HORN	BUIST	REMARKS
Far Ear	Near Ear				
				W T far rib	Cheviot stock
				Ⓛ near rib	Do.
				S L far rib	Do.
				Ⓜ far side	Do.
				T far rib	Do.
		D		Ⓓ near rib	Blackfaced Ewes & Cross Lambs
		D		Ⓓ far rib	Do.
			D	**D** far rib	Badlieu, Tweedhopefoot, and Glencragie burned with **W T** before 1907
			D	**D** near rib	

Index

A

Algiers 173
Allen, Peter 17, 20
Anderson family, neighbours at
    Hearthstane 11, 95, 97, 102
Anderson, Andrew of Glenveg 167, 168,
    169, 170
Anderson, Archie, Jim's father 93, 144
Anderson, Helen 169
Anderson, Jamie, a retired herd 175
Anderson, Janet 169
Anderson, Jim, boyhood friend of
    Andrew Lorimer 11, 12, 14, 15, 25,
    28, 32, 34, 50, 64, 75, 79, 92, 136
Annan 57
Annandale 61
Annan Water 61, 105, 115
Arthur, Lady 173
Atherstane 1, 7

B

Badenteric 60
Badlieu 29, 59, 65, 72, 77, 98, 100, 102,
    126, 136, 168, 178
Balamans Hill 105
Balfour, F. R. S. 142
Bamfleet 165
Barns 80
Battle of Culloden 50
Battle of Rullion Green 60
Beech Glade 30
Belgium 30
Bell, Geordie 107, 109
Bield Burn 25
Bield Cottage 30
Bield Scaur 124
Bield, the 42, 53, 115, 163, 199
Biggar 34, 79, 80, 100, 103, 106, 109,
    165, 197
Biggar Auction Market 4
Biggar Curling Club 198
Binnie, a gamekeeper 155, 156
Black, Mr, farmer at Wandel 4, 10
Blacklaw 138
Blockade, German 30

Blyth Bridge 2, 4, 6, 95
Bonnie Bertha of Badlieu 49, 60
Bower of Polmood 53
Braid Law 54, 186, 187
Broad Law 24
Broadlaw 66, 142
Broughton 38, 44, 45, 46, 52, 54, 65,
    111, 114, 115, 116, 120, 128, 138, 140,
    144, 153, 156, 164, 165, 175, 195
Broughton Curling Club 198
Broughton Free Kirk 164
Broughton Post Office 30
Brown, Alec 30, 172
Brown, Dominie 172, 195
Brown, James, 'Jimmie', herd in
    Tweedsmuir x, 77, 124–126, 170, 172,
    175, 186
Brown, Mary Kerr, Mrs Millar,
    mother-in-law of Andrew Lorimer
    172, 173, 175
Brown, Will, fiddler 181
Brown, William 172
Buchan, John 164
Buchan, Rev William, father of John
    Buchan 6
Burnetland 165
Burns, Robert 49

C

Caldwell, Jane, mother of Andrew
    Lorimer 1, 101
Caledonian Forest 79
Cameron, Barbara, first wife of Andrew
    Lorimer x, 53
Cameron, John 53
Cameron, Willie 166
Canada 172
Canadian Expeditionary Force 30
Canmore, Malcolm 49
Cappercleugh 104
Carlareen 55
Carlavin Hill 86
Carlisle 61, 122
Carlowes Brig (see Tweedsmuir bridge)
Carluke 7

Carnegie, Andrew 16
Carrick, Geordie 110, 111, 113
Carruthers, John, of Fruid 195
Carterhope 57, 61, 105, 165, 183
Chapel Kingledores 52
Charles I 47
Chester Knowes 60
Chester Lees 60
Christmas 11
Cleugh, the 165, 167
Cloverhill 6
Clyde, the 60
Clydeside 97
Coats, Lady 173
Cockiland 162
Colville's Ironworks 125
Cor Water 59
Coronation of King George V 11
Covenanters 50
Cox, Graham 47
Craig Kingledores 52
Craigie Middens 183
Craiglaw 78
Cramalt 8, 50
Crawford, earls of 59
Crockett, Rev W S 19, 49
Cromwell, Oliver 47
Crook 24, 98
Crook Brae 19
Crook farm 53
Crook Inn 8, 35, 44, 53, 79, 100, 166,
     168, 198, 199
Crook, the 64, 165
Crooked Bank 50, 137
Crookhaugh Cottages 53
Curry, G 17

D

Dalkeith Fair 80
David I, 57
Dawyck 7, 80, 142
Dempster, Adam 160–161
Dempster, Tom 196, 198
Department of Agriculture 156
Devil's Beef Tub 50, 115, 140
Dick, Rev. John 196, 197, 198
Dickson, John 48, 109
Dirleton 156
Disruption, the 46
Dollar Law 54
Douglas Estate 151
Douglas, Col. James 50
Down Tweed 66

Dreva 4, 7, 8, 10, 63
Druid's Circle 59
Drumelzier 7, 8, 10, 45, 47, 63, 65, 132
Drumelzier, barony of 59
Drumelzier Place 172
Dumfriesshire 105, 106
Dykehead 161, 198

E

Earlshaugh 105
Earlshaugh farm 59
East Fortune 193
East Linton 193
Easter Happrew 6
Edinburgh 47, 55, 125, 130, 150, 156,
     160, 162, 188, 191
Edinburgh and District Water Trustees
     55, 114
Ellerscleuch Burn 56
Elsrickle 1
Eshiels 44
Ettrick Bridge 35

F

Falkirk Tryst 80
Fingland 30, 59, 63, 72, 132, 168
Flanders 40
Fleming family 52, 58
Fleming, Alexander 195
Flood of 1884 8
'Flu epidemic of 1918 12
Forbes, Lady 50
Forest Curling Club 198
Forest Hill 4
Forestry Commission 49, 52, 142, 150
Forth Railway Bridge 63
Fraser family 52, 57
Fraser, Sir Simon 52, 57
French, John 183
Fruid 24, 28, 35, 54, 56, 57, 59, 61, 62,
     66, 72, 89, 103, 105, 114, 116, 120,
     129, 130, 132, 133, 140, 148, 151, 165,
     172, 183
Fruid Lakes 25, 89, 130, 150

G

Gala Burn 23, 106
Gala Burn Wood 22, 23, 138
Galloway 60
Gameshope 55, 57, 109, 141, 162, 167,
     168, 169
Gameshope Burn 55, 89
Garelet 55, 89, 139, 166, 183

Giant's Stones 59
Glasgow Fair 127, 145
Glebe, the 163
Glenbrec 24
Glenbreck 30, 59, 61, 72, 107, 176
Glencothco 38
Glencraigs Burn 105, 132
Glenheurie 51, 66, 79, 133, 137
Glenheurie Rig 36
Glenholm 45, 61, 81
Glenriskie 24, 53, 66, 102, 175
Glenveg 10, 53, 107, 126, 167, 168, 169, 170
Gosland 165
Green Syke 61
Green, the, inn 164, 165
Gretna 43
Gunn, Mr 199
Guthrie, Dr James 4

H
Hamildean 2, 6, 91
Hamilton, Duchess of 151
Hart Fell 54, 56, 183
Haswellsykes 80
Hawk Linn 56, 141, 183
Hawkshaw 59, 60, 63, 72, 132
Hay family 52, 55, 58
Hays of Drumelzier 52
Hazelbush Hill 142
Hearthstane 11, 12, 24, 28, 29, 30, 40, 44, 52, 54, 55, 58, 63, 65, 70, 71, 77, 79, 80, 81, 82, 92, 93, 94, 95, 101, 102, 110, 120, 122, 126, 129, 133, 136, 151, 152, 163, 167, 168, 184, 187
Hearthstane bridge 24, 34, 35, 63, 64, 120, 121
Hearthstane farm ix, 11, 14, 40, 43, 53, 66
Hearthstane woods 16
Hill Herd 48
Hog Hill Wood 137
Hogg, James 51
Holmswater 80, 140
Home Defence Unit 191
Home Guard 30, 44, 191
Hopecarton 45, 52, 80
Hopehead 138, 168, 170
Hunter family 59
Hunter, Adam 50
Hunter, Alexander 50
Hunter, John 19
Hunter, John of Polmood 50

Hunter, Robert 50
Hunter's Holes 50, 51
Hutton Curling Club 198

I
Inveraray Castle 173

K
Kennedy family, 106, 107
Kennel Club 151
Kerr, Jimmy 128
Kilbucho, 45, 80, 81, 167
Kilbucho Place 165
Kilmarnock 43
Kilpotlees 11
Kingledores 7, 20, 24, 30, 38, 52, 79, 98, 138, 170, 182
Kingledores Burn 52 116
Kingledores Hope 52
Kingledores Hopehead 24, 61, 170, 186
Kingussie hotel 166
Kitchener, Lord 43
Knights Templar 54

L
Laidlaw, Will 81
Lanark 80, 81
Lang, Andrew 126
Lang, Jean 126, 127
Lang, Miss 35, 169
Lauder, Harry 40
Lawson, Jamie 30
Lily Bank 22
Lindsay family 59
Lindsay of Dreva 8
Lindsay, Margaret 170
Lindsay, Mr of Stanhope 199
Lindsay, William 48
Linkumdoddie 49
Linn Brig (see Tweedsmuir bridge)
Linn Pool 16, 122, 127
Linn, the 62
Little, Mick 81
Loch Craig Head 54
Loch Leven 127
Loch Skeen 141
Lochmaben 107
Logan 46, 47, 80, 109, 115
Lorimer, Janet, sister of Andrew Lorimer 101, 169
Lorimer, Jim, brother of Andrew Lorimer 40, 42, 43
Lorimer, Margaret 'Peg', eldest sister of

Andrew Lorimer 165
Lorimer, Thomas, father of Andrew ix, 2, 100, 101
Lorimer, William, grandfather of Andrew Lorimer 4
Lyne 6
Lyne Water 2

M

Manor Bridge 80
Manor Valley 170
Manse 25, 40
Martyr's Grave 19
Mary Stuart 55
Mason, Dr 101
Masterton family 53, 164, 166
Masterton, Ebenezer 164, 166
Masterton, Helen 164
Masterton, James 164
Masterton, John 164
Masterton, Mr 42
McMorran, Mary, grandmother of Andrew Lorimer 4
McMorran, shepherd 105
Megget 8, 50, 66, 81, 86, 104, 167, 186
Meggethead 8, 81
Melrose, monks of 45, 52
Melville, Mrs, farmer at Wandel 10
Menzion 28, 30, 58, 66, 71, 72, 89, 106, 114, 132, 147, 151, 160, 163, 172, 182, 184
Menzion Burn 57
Menzion Knows 187
Merlindale Bridge 10
Miller, Margaret Lindsay, second wife of Andrew Lorimer x
Minister, the 39
Mitchell, Houston 50
Moffat 43, 44, 103, 105, 115, 140
Moffat Agricultural Show 115
Moffat Curling Club 198
Moffat Hydropathic 115
Moffat Water 26, 141
Mons 30
Montgomery, James 47
Moor Foot 82
Moray House x, 152
Mossfennan x, 4, 6, 45, 46, 47, 52, 61, 98, 107, 109, 145, 155, 156, 157, 175, 188
Motherwell 125
Motte Burn 66
Murray family 47

Murray, Dave
Murray, David 47
Murray, John of Broughton 50
Murray, Sir David of Stanhope 50, 58
Murray, Sir David, 4th baronet 47
Murray, Veronica, wife of Robert Hunter 50
Murray, William 47

N

Nether Fruid 183
New Zealand forces 35
Newbigging, William 114, 115
Norman's Castle 48
North Berwick 156, 189

O

Old Hall 42
Old Talla 89
Oliver 40, 53, 61, 77, 163, 170, 172, 181, 186, 196
Oliver Castle 50, 54, 57
Oliver Castle, barony of 52
Oliver Cottage 170, 172
Over Menzion 89, 168, 182, 183

P

Paisley 173
Parritch Cairn 110
Patervan 24, 49, 52, 63, 72, 77, 80
Pattison, Mrs 189, 191, 193
Peebles x, 44, 45, 65, 80, 81, 102, 105, 115, 155
Peebles Curling Club 198
Peebles High School x, 45, 140, 144, 165
Peeblesshire 90, 151
Poletti, Danny 103, 104
Polmood 49, 50, 52, 60, 63, 66, 80, 98, 138
Polmood Burn 52, 133
Polmood Craig 186
Polskene 60
Poor Law 187
Porteous family 59
Priesthope 57
Purveys, William 45

Q

Quarter Hill 147
Quilt Burn 7, 35

R

Rachan, 175

Rachan pond 197
Ragged Schools 4
Red Cross 40, 193
Reevers Road 57, 61
Reive, James 104, 105
Renwick family 76
Riggs, the 168, 175, 176
River Tay 122
River Tweed 1, 24, 25, 27, 36, 45, 49,
    53, 54, 56, 59, 61, 63, 66, 80, 95, 98,
    106, 114, 120, 122, 126, 128, 130, 133,
    142, 145, 163, 175
Robb, 'Stumpy' 120
Roberton 11
Robertson, John 89, 166
Robertson, Ned, of Holmshill 38
Roman road 60
Romans 60
Rosebery family 82
Rosebery, Lord 82
Ross, Ritchie 114, 115, 163, 164, 169
Rowan Bank 110, 160
Royal Caledonian Curling Club 199

S
Sargasso Sea 124, 132
Saughton gaol 188
Scaur Water 166
School Board 17
Scots Guards 42
Sharpe, David 166
Shaw, Bell 176
Sinclair, Mr 198
Sked, T, pest officer 133
Skinner, Scott 40
Skirling Fair 80
Smith, Ally 34
Smith, Jack 2, 7
Solway, the 60
Somme, the 43
Soonhope x, 44, 102, 155
South America 30
Southern Reporter 48
Spoot Heids 183
St Mary's Loch 8
Stanhope 47, 48, 49, 52, 63, 106, 182,
    187
Stanhope Brae 115, 160
Stanhope Treasure 48
Stevenston 2
Stewart, Mr 116
Stobo 65, 98
Stodart, Mr T 196, 198

Strawberry Hill 57
Stuart family 52
Stuart, Walter of Kingledores 199
Sunday School 26
Sun Valley, USA 172
Swire 80
Syart 81
Symington 81

T
Talla 47, 54, 55, 56, 57, 62, 66, 72, 86,
    89, 103, 105, 114, 116, 120, 126, 127,
    160, 162, 163, 166, 172, 175, 181, 182
Talla Banks 89
Talla Burn 20, 128
Talla Dam 41, 45, 120, 130, 132, 162,
    174, 181
Talla Glen 24
Talla Lakes 169
Talla Linnfoot 24
Talla Linns 55
Talla railway 24, 43, 175, 187
Talla reservoir ix, 24, 45, 133
Thorburn family 30
Thorburn, Mr, owner of Hearthstane
    14, 35, 52, 115, 126
Thorburn, Billy 30
Thorburn, Jamie 30
Thorburn, Nancy 14
Thorburn, Robert 30
Thorburn, Vincent 30
Thorburn, William 77
Titanic 14
Tod, Jimmie 41
Todd, Willie, fiddler 181
Tory party 174
Tudhope, Miss, of Broughton Place 165
Turnbull, James 7
Turnbull, Mrs, of Quilt Burn 32
Tweed 7, 8, 10, 103, 105, 107, 109, 116,
    124, 126, 132, 172, 186
Tweed Commission 124
Tweed Valley 47
Tweedhopefoot 17, 59, 168
Tweedie family 52, 54
Tweedie-Stodart family 54
Tweedie-Stodart, Mary 162
Tweedshaws farm 59, 168
Tweedsmuir 24, 25, 30, 44, 45, 47, 58,
    61, 71, 79, 80, 81, 89, 103, 106, 107,
    114, 115, 124, 128, 148, 152, 156, 157,
    163, 165, 166, 168, 170, 174, 175, 176,
    181, 182

Tweedsmuir Bridge 27, 54, 62, 63, 123, 127, 163, 170, 181
Tweedsmuir Church x, 50
Tweedsmuir churchyard 19, 170
Tweedsmuir Curling Club 161, 195, 198, 199
Tweedsmuir parish 11, 52
Tweedsmuir school 15, 45, 151, 172
Tyninghame 190

U
Up Tweed 66, 132, 133
Upper Drumelzier 52
Upper Tweed Valley x, 45, 54, 135, 150, 176

V
Vietch, James 7

W
Wandel ix, 4, 10, 35, 167
War Savings Scheme 192
Watt, John 132, 175
'Wee Davie' 35

Welsh family 46
Welsh, Rev Dr William 4
Welsh, Rev William 46
Welsh, Robert 45–46
Wemyss, Earl of 137
West Linton 115
White Comb 54, 141
White Rig Wood 80, 138
Whitekirk x, 189, 193
Whitekirk School 192, 193, 194
Wisdom Pool 98, 121
Women's Rural Institute (WRI) 189, 193
Woodend 167
World War I x, 30–44, 90, 105, 107, 124, 135, 162, 163, 172, 181, 182
World War II x, 66, 133, 162, 189
Wormald, the 47
Wrae, 38, 144

Y
Yarrow 8
Yellowlees, Janet 17, 20
Yellowlees, John 17, 30, 199